The New Frontier Investors

Jagdeep Singh Bachher • Adam D. Dixon • Ashby H.B. Monk

The New Frontier Investors

How Pension Funds, Sovereign Funds, and
Endowments are Changing the Business of
Investment Management and Long-Term Investing

palgrave
macmillan

Jagdeep Singh Bachher
University of California
California, USA

Ashby H.B. Monk
Stanford University
Stanford, California, USA

Adam D. Dixon
University of Bristol
Bristol, United Kingdom

ISBN 978-1-137-50856-0   ISBN 978-1-137-50857-7   (eBook)
DOI 10.1057/978-1-137-50857-7

Library of Congress Control Number: 2016941881

This Palgrave Macmillan imprint is published by Springer Nature
The registered company is Macmillan Publishers Ltd. London

For
Harbhajan, Kuldip, Aradhana, Jaspreet, Meher and Prabhnoor—JSB
Olga, Fay and Juno—ADD
Courtney, Henry and Bea—AHBM

Preface

The global financial services industry has been the subject of criticism since the 2008–2009 financial crisis. From social movements such as Occupy Wall Street to the economic elites at the World Economic Forum, there is widespread concern that the leading edge of the financial services industry has lost sight of its objective function: to facilitate the efficient allocation of economic resources over space and time under conditions of risk and uncertainty. Instead, the investment houses of the leading international financial centres (IFCs) often seem to be working in their own interests, even destroying rather than creating value for clients, shareholders, and the real economy. For some, parts of the financial world have become socially dysfunctional.[1] Simultaneously, short-termism appears pervasive, driven by structural changes such as mark-to-market accounting coupled with cognitive constraints to long-term decision making and herd behaviour. Consequently, existential socioeconomic challenges that are material to the generation of value over the long term, such as demographic ageing and climate change, are secondary concerns for many in the financial community, if they are a concern at all.

There are, however, two important yet understudied and unmapped developments challenging the global geography of finance and investment. First, large institutional investors with long time horizons are appearing in cities outside of the IFCs that have little or no history as purveyors of flows of global finance. This is due in large part to the dramatic growth and emergence of sovereign wealth funds in places such as Abu Dhabi, Auckland, Beijing, Edmonton, Juneau, Moscow and Oslo. Indeed, more sovereign funds have

---

[1] See, Adair Turner, 'What banks do, what should they do and what public policies are needed to ensure best result for the real economy?' (Cass Business School, 2010).

been set up in the past decade than in all the years before.² Second, a community of long time horizon institutional investors, which includes sovereign funds but also public pension funds, family offices, foundations and endowments, is pushing back against the misaligned incentives, high fees, poor returns and short-termism embedded in the for-profit asset management industry, which the financial crisis brought to the fore.

This growing group of long-term beneficiary institutions, which we define as *frontier investors*, is taking back responsibility for the end-to-end management of their investment portfolios by insourcing some asset management and reconceptualizing the investment decision-making process to bypass for-profit service providers and, in some cases, IFCs, altogether. Our work in the industry and our academic research covering sovereign funds, public pension funds, foundations, family offices and endowements from North America, Europe, the Middle East, Africa, Australasia and East Asia, suggests that frontier investors are developing ways of overcoming their geographic constraints. They have begun to harness network economies where financial services agglomeration economies are not present, and are leveraging their locational and organizational attributes to meet their human resources needs. This shift in practice and organizational form has potentially significant implications for the global geography of finance and the allocation of capital across time and space.

Our findings do not, however, suggest the demise of IFCs and the for-profit financial service providers. Financial centres produce a range of agglomeration economies in addition to offering complementary services that many frontier investors in financial outposts cannot. Attracting and retaining talented and specialized workers, and accessing sufficient and attractive deal flows, are easier to achieve in an urban agglomeration. Hence, at this juncture, there is an insufficient critical mass of organizations that are successfully and efficiently overcoming the organizational and geographical constraints necessary to threaten the dominance of the IFCs and the for-profit service providers. But we'd like to see that change. If *frontier finance*, the term we give to this innovation in asset management, represents a window of locational opportunity, it is in its infancy. And even if frontier finance is unable to unseat the dominance of IFCs, it may over time come to represent a viable (if small in comparison) parallel, decentralized system of global finance that provides a better alignment between the owners and users of capital, as the rents that would normally acrue to intermediaries and other market participants (e.g. short-term speculators) are removed.

---

² For an extended treatment of sovereign funds see, G.L. Clark, et al., SOVEREIGN WEALTH FUNDS: LEGITIMACY, GOVERNANCE, AND GLOBAL POWER (Princeton University Press, 2013).

At the core, we are interested in studying frontier finance and understanding frontier investors because they are constrained by their geographies and, as a result, forced to be innovative to operate effectively. Within the long-term investor community, innovation can be an overwhelming challenge, stymied by prudent person rules, peer risk and governance rules. Indeed, for these institutional investors to find a more aligned access point to the financial services industry, they have had to develop capabilities and resources that are not standard among other asset owners. How and why they have done this is of critical importance to this book. If we are to reconstruct the long-term investment community for long-term success, it starts by adopting innovative and creative techniques that are rarely recognised as being innovative or creative. How many public pension funds would you, the reader, describe as innovative? And yet, these long-term investors form the base of our capitalist system, setting the incentives for all the other agents operating in the global economy. In our view, the base of capitalism should be more capitalist, and that will require doing things differently in the future.

The nine chapters that follow are critical as well as constructive. In Chap. 1 we provide an outline the contemporary geography of investment management to help explain why most beneficiary financial institutions are dependent on third-party service providers. While this chapter has an academic tone, it is important for understanding the constraints that large beneficiary institutions face in becoming more independent and resourceful organizations, We argue that these constraints are partly a function of geography. But an organization's history and geography are no excuse for complacency. Yes, place matters. Yet, as we show in subsequent chapters, there are innovations that minimize, and in some cases eliminate, the limitations that many large beneficiary institutions face. We firmly believe that there is a wealth of opportunity for action, whether at a public pension fund in the middle of the United States or a sovereign fund in central Asia, to unleash their structural advantage and long time horizons in support of sustainable economic growth and shared prosperity.

Investment management is all about producing returns. Organizations receive money to which processes, people and informational advantages are added. These three factors of production are supposed to produce returns. In Chaps. 2 and 3 we outline what beneficiary investors can do to improve the investment process and attract the compelling and diverse set of people necessary for producing returns in an uncertain and globalized world economy. Improving process—or rather investment governance—begins by understanding the constraints and capabilities of an organization; establishing investment beliefs to guide decision-making; and providing the investment process with the resources of time and attention that it needs. Frontier investors are often in the hinterlands of global financial markets where the talent pool is limited, even though they may actually be on the immediate environs of cities such as New York and London. Yet, as we have discovered, some beneficiary institutions have figured out how to attract best and brightest no matter where they are located.

Chapters 4 and 5 focus on the benefits of collaboration with like-minded beneficiary institutions and the possibilities for geographic expansion—or rather the establishment of satellite offices in major financial centres or important commercial cities. In both cases it is about unleashing structural advantage, whether that means bringing together investors that are spread across the globe to take advantage of each one's unique organizational and place-based attributes, or placing teams in the heart of the market to monitor investments and build more aligned partnerships with the financial services industry. In Chap. 6 we further the discussion on collaboration, providing insight on collaboration among long-term investors with venture capitalists.

In Chap. 7, we turn our attention to transparency. For many long-term investors full transparency is a legal requirement and not a choice. Although we believe in the moral and democratic imperatives underlying transparency and in the economic efficiency that should result, being transparent for the long-term investor can be problematic. Transparency may, unfortunately, drive short-term behaviour and myopic decision-making, at the expense of long-term performance. Furthermore, transparency may hinder a move towards a more capable and innovative investment organization. It is easier to follow the herd than to seek out new frontiers. But we think transparency is multi-faceted. It is much more than simply short-term performance metrics. Using the context of the crisis of international legitimacy that beset sovereign wealth funds in the last decade, we offer a nuanced perspective of the different forms of transparency and how such an understanding can help long-term investors explain how they invest and how they operate as an innovative and capable investment organization.

In the penultimate chapter, we take a slightly different turn in our narrative to consider sovereign development funds, particularly for developing countries. Indeed, the world has become too interconnected and interdependent for us to limit our discussion to large beneficiary institutions in rich countries. Not only are developing countries an important investment destination, many are turning to state-sponsored investment funds to encourage economic growth and development. We think these investment funds have the potential to become frontier investors. Some of these sovereign funds in resource-rich countries are basic stabilization funds invested in low-risk assets abroad. Others have established funds with specific mandates to generate economic capabilities at home. Although we are sympathetic of this new class of frontier investor, we also recognize the challenges and risks that can impede their success. As such, we outline principles and policies that support success. And although the thrust of the chapter concerns developing countries, these same principles apply to any institutional investor that takes seriously the development of the real economy.

In place of a conventional conclusion, the final chapter presents the 10 pillars of centennial performance that we are using to guide the University of California's Office of the Chief Investment Officer. These principles and policies emerged from the same material that informs the chapters of this book. We take the opportunity with this chapter to demonstrate how seriously we take the lessons learned from our research and experience engaging with other frontier investors. We are putting our words into action.

Oakland, Bristol and Stanford

Jagdeep Singh Bachher
Adam D. Dixon
Ashby H.B. Monk
March 2016

Acknowledgements

The themes in this book cross continents, they bring together ideas from several academic disciplines, and they are informed by practical experience in the field. As such, this book is as much a collaborative effort among the authors as it is a reflection of the invaluable insight and experience of the many people whom we have had the privilege of meeting in our research. In particular, we would like to thank Gordon L. Clark who has been a mentor and generator of ideas, as well as a co-author on a previous publication that informs Chap. 6. We would also like to thank Kiran Sridhar, who also contributed to that section, as well as Qais Al-Kharusi who contributed to a paper that informed Chap. 5, and Peter Clark for contributions to ideas developed in Chap. 8. Special thanks are reserved for Raymond Levitt, director of the Global Projects Center at Stanford, who never lost sight of the merit and necessity of the project, always showing immense excitement and solidarity. We would also like to acknowledge Rajiv Sharma, Dane Rook, Elliott Donnelley, Derek Murphy, Lindsay Holden, Mike Bennon, Tom Welsh, Leo De Bever, Duncan Sinclair, Allan Wain, and Randy Humpaleg.

Some of the arguments put forth in this book draw, in part, on ideas and material that were developed in previously published articles. We wish to acknowledge the publishers of the original sources: Taylor and Francis for Adam D. Dixon and Ashby H.B. Monk (2014), 'Frontier finance', *Annals of the Association of American Geographers*, 104(4), pp. 852–868; Adam D. Dixon and Ashby H.B. Monk (2012), 'Reconciling transparency and long-term investing within sovereign funds', *Journal of Sustainable Finance & Investment*, 2(3–4), 275–286; Adam D. Dixon and Ashby H. B. Monk (2014), 'Financializing development: toward a sympathetic critique of sovereign development funds', *Journal of Sustainable Finance & Investment*, 4(4),

357–371; Rotman School of Management for Jagdeep S. Bachher and Ashby H. B. Monk (2013), 'Platforms and vehicles for institutional co-investing', *Rotman International Journal of Pension Management*, 6(1), 64–71; Chartered Alternative Investment Analyst Association for Jagdeep S. Bachher, Gordon L. Clark, Ashby H. B. Monk, and Kiran Sridha (2014), 'The "valley of opportunity": rethinking venture capital for long-term institutional investors', *Alternative Investment Analyst Review*, 3(1), 63–75.

Jagdeep Singh Bachher has contributed to this book in a personal capacity. Any views expressed in this book do not necessarily reflect those of current or former employers

Contents

1   **The Foundations of Capitalism: Beneficiary Asset Managers**   1
    Pension Fund Capitalism   2
    Sovereign Fund Capitalism   5
    The Geography of Finance   7
        Large Frontier Cities   10
        Centres of Global Finance   11
        Small Cities on the Distant Frontier   11
        Small Cities on the Frontier   12
    Conclusions   13

2   **Unleashing Innovation Through Better Governance**   15
    What's Your Mission?   17
    What Do You Believe In?   18
    What Is Your Comparative Advantage?   19
    How Do You Develop Investment Beliefs?   20
        Limit Focus   21
    Investing in Governance   24
    Conclusions   27

3   **Unleashing Innovation Through People**   29
    Why Is it Hard to Find the Right People?   30
    Green, Grey, Grounded   31
    Tomorrow's Strategy: 'Moneyball'   34
    Conclusions   37

4 **Unleashing Innovation Through Collaboration**   39
   The Benefits and Challenges of Collaboration   40
   The Cleantech Syndicate   42
     Motivation   42
     Structure   44
     Responsibilities   44
     Investments   44
     Implementation   45
   A Path Forward   47
   Setting Up Co-investment Vehicles and Platforms   48
     The Alliance   48
     The Syndicate   49
     The Seed   50
     The Choice   50
   Conclusions   51

5 **Unleashing Locational Advantage**   53
   The Goals of Geographic Expansion   55
     International Financial Centres   55
     Non-financial Centres   58
   The Challenges of Geographic Expansion   59
     International Finance Centres   59
     Non-financial Centres   60
   Geographic Expansion: Key Lessons   61
     Governance and Culture   61
     Alignment with Fund Strategy   62
     Setting Goals   62
     Staffing   63
     Politics   63
     Scalability   64
   Conclusions   64

6 **The Valley of Opportunity: Bringing Innovation
   to Venture Capital**   67
   The Valley of Death   69
   The Valley of Opportunity   73
   The Innovation Alliance   74
     Success Factors   76

Lessons Learned	76
Principles	77
Policies	79
Conclusions	79

7   Does Transparency Restrict Innovation Among Long-term Investors? 81

Threatening the Status Quo?	84
Transparency and Long-term Investing	87
Aspects of Transparency	91
Two Views of Transparency	94
Conclusions	95

8   Catalyzing Development in a Short-term World 97

Sovereign Fund Solutions	100
Macroeconomic Stability	100
Productive Efficiency	102
Distributive Justice	106
A Basic Typology	107
People and Organizational Design	108
Two Views of Finance	110
Intersecting Politics	111
Principles, Policies and Pitfalls	112
Principles of Governance	113
Policies of Management	114
Pitfalls to Avoid	115
Conclusions	116

9   Ten Pillars for Centennial Outperformance 119

The Pillars of Our Future Success	122
Pillar 1: Less Is More	122
Pillar 2: Risk Rules Everything	123
Pillar 3: Concentration	124
Pillar 4: Creativity Pays Dividends	126
Pillar 5: Putting Information into Action	127
Pillar 6: A Committed Team	128
Pillar 7: The UC Advantage	129

Pillar 8: Execution and Alignment   130
Pillar 9: Leveraging Technology   131
Pillar 10: Centennial Performance   132
Final Thoughts   133

Bibliography   135

Index   141

List of Figures

Fig. 1.1	Pension fund capitalism	3
Fig. 1.2	Sovereign fund capitalism	6
Fig. 1.3	The geography of finance	9
Fig. 2.1	Risk budget and governance budget synchronization	26
Fig. 2.2	Alternative representation of governance budget and performance	26
Fig. 8.1	Sovereign development fund strategies	105

List of Tables

Table 5.1   Satellite office formation   56
Table 7.1   Framing transparency   92

List of Boxs

Box 2.1 Translating Market Dominance into Competitive Advantage
         at APG   19
Box 2.2 Investment Beliefs for the Chief Investment Officer of the Regents   23
Box 3.1 Attracting and Retaining Skilled Workers in Edmonton   33

1

The Foundations of Capitalism: Beneficiary Asset Managers

In its purest form, the financial system is simply the interface between people and entities that have capital and those that require capital, under conditions of risk and uncertainty. There are temporal dimensions as well as spatial dimensions. The parties concerned are probably working to different time scales and are likely to be dispersed geographically. Financial centres and a financial services industry emerge to intermediate and match these differences. If this is done efficiently, holders of capital earn a return for providing their capital to users of capital. These users put the money to use, whether it is to expand a company, building a bridge, or invest in the health and well-being of a nation. Everyone wins. And for facilitating these flows, intermediaries are paid a fee. These fees are supposed to cover the cost of infrastructure required to move the funds around and to reward the people who identify the most efficient and promising allocation of capital.

Many asset owners are starting to question how much they are paying for this service. They are questioning having to pay fees just to access a service, regardless of performance, as if they depended on the service and not the other way around. Indeed, parts of the financial services industry seem to have forgotten that it is the asset owners that provide the capital that sustains their business model. This isn't right. If the purpose of the financial system is forgotten, it is ultimately unsustainable. Unfortunately, many asset owners have become dependent on an industry and service that, at least in some parts, has forgotten who works for whom. The dependency that has arisen has a number of explanations, from regulatory and political

© The Editor(s) (if applicable) and The Author(s) 2016
J. Singh Bachher et al., *The New Frontier Investors*,
DOI 10.1057/978-1-137-50857-7_1

constraints to the availability of skilled workers and a lack of options. Many are dependent likewise because of where they are located: far from the markets they need to employ their capital.

In this chapter we outline the map of large beneficiary institutions, focusing on sovereign funds and public pension funds, and the functional and spatial structure of asset ownership and asset management. In our view, these asset owners, as well as endowments, represent a critical base of our capitalist system; the source from which investment capital ultimately begins its path to productive capital. Here, we note that external delegation dominates convention. We then provide a conceptual model of frontier places, as a means of clarifying the relationship between asset owners in such locations and international financial centres (IFCs). The final section concludes.

Pension Fund Capitalism

In the twentieth century, the accumulation and pooling of wealth was a consequence of what could be described as pension fund capitalism. This is primarily a developed-world phenomenon, whereby Anglo-American countries and others such as Finland, Switzerland, Japan and the Netherlands made prefunded pensions, both public and private, important components of their respective pension systems. With successive pension reforms driving the growth of capitalized pension arrangements in other advanced economies (e.g. Germany) and the growth of pension savings in middle income economies, pension assets continue to grow in size and in geographic origin.[1]

At the end of 2014, global pension assets in the seventeen largest pension markets stood at $36,023 billion, according to data from the 2014 P&I/Towers Watson World 300. While, collectively, retirement-income organizations represent a major component of global financial markets, there are a number of institutions that, individually, control significant amounts of financial assets, which places them apart from smaller pools of capital in their ability to innovate as organizations and confront asymmetric power relationships in the investment management industry.

Figure 1.1 shows the largest retirement-income organizations with assets greater than $25 billion.[2] The majority shown are public employee pension

---

[1] A. D. Dixon, *The rise of pension fund capitalism in Europe: an unseen revolution?*, 13 New Political Economy (2008).

[2] In the P&I/Towers Watson World 300 the Norwegian GPF-G is included as a pension fund. While the government changed the name from 'petroleum' fund to 'pension' fund, and has stated that the fund will cover pension liabilities, the GPF-G far outweighs any future pension liabilities. Hence, we include the

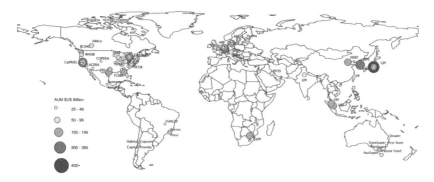

Fig. 1.1 Pension fund capitalism

plans, and thus government sponsored, that provide guaranteed income streams to their beneficiaries at retirement. There are, however, single-employer corporate sponsored pension funds and multiemployer industry funds. The latter are common in the Netherlands and other continental European countries. Many of the single-employer funds are associated with former state-owned enterprises and/or monopoly utilities, such as the BT Group and the Electricity Supply Pension in the United Kingdom, or legacy manufacturing firms, such as General Motors and Ford, in the United States. The General Motors pension fund, for example, is a separate asset management company located in New York. Included also are large pension reserve funds such as the French *Fonds de réserve pour la retraite* and the Australian Future Fund, the latter of which was formed to cover the government's liabilities for promised public sector pensions. Where there is a concentration of funds in a particular region, labels are not provided or only the largest fund is labelled (e.g. Tokyo).

As expected, large funds are mainly present in countries with a history of pre-funded occupational pensions. In Europe, the largest pension funds are in the Netherlands, Denmark and the UK. In North America, large pension funds are located in population centres of the US Northeast and Midwest; Ontario, Canada; and several US public employee funds in places such as California, Florida, Texas and the Pacific Northwest. The largest pension fund in the world is the Government Pension Investment Fund of Japan, which manages roughly $1.4 trillion in reserve funds of the Employees' Pension Insurance and the National Pension. There are also other large pension funds based in Tokyo, such as the

---

GPF-G in Fig. 1.2 as a sovereign wealth fund. We also include the Alberta Investment Management Company (AIMCo) in Fig. 1.1, even though it also manages the Alberta Heritage Savings Trust Fund, which is also included in Fig. 1.2. The majority of AIMCo funds under management come from public pension funds in Alberta.

Local Government Officials pension fund and the Pension Fund Association, which is a multiemployer pension fund. Elsewhere in the Asia region are the large provident funds of Singapore and Malaysia, and notably, the National Pension Service of Korea, which has just over $300 billion in assets under management.

In using a cutoff of $25 billion to simplify the map and highlight the largest pension funds, many smaller public sector pension funds across the US are excluded, and, more importantly, the concentration (and visual overlap) of smaller pension funds in particular cities. As a result, some of the largest pension fund markets in terms of assets to gross domestic product (GDP) that we have not already mentioned are understated. For example, with compulsory pension savings in Chile, there is a large asset management industry in Santiago. This is likewise the case for Australia where compulsory pension savings feeds a fund management industry centred in Sydney and Melbourne.

Although the spatial structure of large retirement-income organizations is dispersed, albeit across predominantly high-income, industrialized countries, it is important to emphasize that for the majority of these organizations asset management is delegated to for-profit private sector asset managers, most of whom are located in international or regional financial centres. Two factors drive this. First, local markets are too small and provide limited opportunities for diversification. The local market can be defined as the national economy, as in the case of the Netherlands or Australia, where the ratio of pension assets to GDP in 2013 was 166 per cent and 103 per cent respectively, or a regional economy, as in the case of Colorado Public Employees Retirement Association.[3] Second, many funds are located in areas where the local market for specialized financial services is limited. We come back to the significance of this later in this chapter.

The main task of the pension plan board of directors is, in most cases, deciding on asset allocation based on risk-return targets and the selection of external asset managers (usually with the help of external pension consultants). Mandates are either given to a range of managers depending on asset class (extensive delegation), or to a smaller set of asset managers (intensive delegation).[4] In either case, contractual arrangements vary over time but are generally contingent on short-term performance metrics, such as exceeding a particular market benchmark (e.g. the S&P 500).

Few retirement-income organizations manage assets internally. Where more conventional organizations do manage some of their assets internally, they are most likely to manage highly rated fixed-income securities, such as US

---

[3] See OECD Global Pension Statistics, available at www.oecd.org/daf/pensions/gps

[4] G. L. Clark, PENSION FUND CAPITALISM (Oxford University Press, 2000).

Treasuries, or blue chip equities. In either of these cases, the decision to manage assets internally is contingent on whether there is sufficient scale to do so. Yet, what is sufficient scale is an empirical issue. The reason for our using a cutoff of $25 billion is that, in our experience, the pension funds that even consider bringing asset management back into the organization generally have assets in excess of this amount. In any case, pension funds that manage assets internally are still unusual. But, this is changing. And those that do, such as in Canada, manage a range of assets, from public equities to real estate and infrastructure.

Sovereign Fund Capitalism

If pension fund capitalism characterized wealth accumulation and capital pooling in the second half of the twentieth century, nowadays we see accumulation and pooling of wealth by additional means, and in a larger set of countries and regions. Notwithstanding the oil price shocks of the 1970s, commodity prices in general over the past decade reached historic highs, driven by rapid economic growth, particularly in Asia and other emerging market economies, and by an insatiable thirst for commodities in the rich world. For those controlling the rents from these resources, whether public or private, the past decade has been a period of massive wealth accumulation. Another source of wealth accumulation has come from current account imbalances in the global economy. Deficit countries, particularly the US, have amassed significant liabilities vis-à-vis surplus countries—namely China.

While much of the wealth accumulation from commodity production or the rebalancing of global economic activity has accrued to private hands, a large portion has also accrued to those governments that control commodity rents, the central banks that accumulate massive foreign exchange reserves, and governments that maintain consistently strong budget surpluses. To be sure, commodity exporters such as Saudi Arabia or export-led *entrepôt* economies such as Singapore have been accumulating wealth in these ways for decades, and have piled it directly back into global markets (and their own). Yet in the past decade, the growth in wealth accruing to states (or states hoarding wealth) has become a larger phenomenon, reaching more and more countries, and specifically emerging and developing economies. If the current form of global capitalism is one marked by financialization, the rapid growth of government-owned investment funds suggests recognition on the part of states of a world that favours holders of financial assets. As such, sovereign wealth funds (SWFs) are a mechanism by which the state can directly access global financial markets, thus providing a certain, if relative, financial influence in the international political economy.

On our count there are at least 60 sovereign funds in operation around the world, with about $5 trillion in assets under management. Figure 1.2 identifies SWFs with at least $5 billion under management. The figures are based on best estimates using publicly available information at the end of 2011. The largest SWFs with more than $400 billion are Norway's GPF-G, the Abu Dhabi Investment Authority and the China Investment Corporation. In the western hemisphere, the largest SWF is the Alaska Permanent Fund followed by the Texas Permanent Education Fund, which was established in 1851, making it one of, if not the oldest SWF in existence. Similar to Fig. 1.1, smaller funds are not shown. This is particularly the case for the Africa region, where there is a growing number of SWFs in operation or in the planning stages.

What is interesting about this phase of state wealth accrual is that some states are establishing distinct institutional investment organizations charged with managing and investing the country's accumulated wealth in financial markets, as distinct from an entry in the treasury's or central bank's balance sheet. In that respect, organizations are given latitude in executing a mandate set by the government as an independent financial institution. The more sophisticated organizations, such as Singapore's Government Investment Corporation, appear to compete, at least in terms of long-term performance, with the world's largest and most competitive asset managers. Like other large beneficiary asset owners, however, most SWFs delegate asset management to for-profit asset management providers in the world's largest IFCs or large regional financial centres. Again, this is largely a function of either the local economy being too small and limited in terms of diversification, and/or the lack of local asset management capabilities.

The implication of the predominance of the delegation model by large beneficiary institutions is that responsibility for putting funds to work in the market

Fig. 1.2   Sovereign fund capitalism

is left to external private agents. As such, just as a principal-agent relationship exists between the asset owner and the managers of firms—an issue of corporate governance—there is an overarching principal–agent relationship between the asset owner and the asset managers. As with any such relationship, the interests between the two parties are not always symmetrical. Asset owners may use incentives to manage principal-agent conflicts, as implied above, which largely come in the form of contracts whose continuation depends on surplus performance against predetermined benchmarks. Some portfolio managers are, however, adept at gaming institutional investors on performance fees. Indeed, separating out skilled managers from unskilled managers borders on the impossible with current compensation mechanisms; instituting clawback provisions or postponing bonuses is thus likewise ineffective.[5] Accordingly, fees paid by asset owners are often excessive.

While individual agency dilemmas exist between individual asset owners and asset managers, it is important to consider that the potential for asymmetrical information and misaligned interests between the wider organizational fields of asset owners (i.e. the beneficiary institutions described here) and for-profit portfolio managers is driven in part by the power resources (e.g., access to specialized labour, complementary services, time-sensitive information flows) that financial services providers obtain as a function of concentrating in financial centres. Put slightly differently, because the capacity to absorb and leverage market-making activity and the benefits of agglomeration is stronger for those organizations located in financial centres, an asymmetric power relationship is produced between those organizations outside the financial centre. This would imply the existence of monopoly privileges for those agents within IFCs, which complicates interest alignment for asset owners located outside IFCs, while making rent extraction possible for for-profit portfolio managers acting within.

The Geography of Finance

To further clarify the geography of the investment management industry at the global scale, we provide a conceptual model for explaining the locational conditions of beneficiary financial institutions and their relationship to IFCs. For practical purposes, IFC is shorthand for global financial markets. This simple conceptual model thus provides a context for understanding the rationale

[5] D. P. Foster and H. P. Young, *Gaming performance fees by portfolio managers*, 125 THE QUARTERLY JOURNAL OF ECONOMICS (2010).

behind many of the innovations discussed in subsequent chapters relating to overcoming geographical constraints. Indeed, conventionally, capital flows from asset owners through a hierarchy of financial centres to the users of capital. While this spatial and functional structure is still relevant, there is potential for working differently. In short, there is an opportunity for asset owners to allocate their capital directly to capital users and through alternative networks of col-labourators and co-investors, some of which may still be located in financial centres. Yet, this requires innovation.

For any knowledge and information-intensive business, of which financial services is included, effective and specialized labour is a key factor in success and survival. Ensuring access to a large and stable supply of specialized work-ers is one reason why competing firms in an industry tend to locate in clusters in urban and regional agglomerations. Search and match costs are lower for firms, and, importantly, the presence of competing employers, which drives up remuneration levels, incentivizes employees to invest in skills upgrading and specialization, whether through further education or by switching between competing firms (which also produces knowledge spillovers). By moving to an IFC, financial workers have a wider variety of firms for which they can work or firms of a sufficient size (e.g. a global investment bank) such that a range of skills can be acquired. As such, workers can develop an extensive skill set by working for a buy-side and a sell-side firm, or an intensive skill set by focusing a career path on a specific investment activity (e.g. commercial real estate).

Just as the labour market is important to financial services firms, so is access to a variety of intermediate service providers, ranging from accounting, audit and legal services, to specialist research firms, and investment consultants. If there is a premium on time, financial services firms locating near these inter-mediate inputs can ensure timely and reliable service. And, as the market for intermediate producer services is likely to be competitive, financial services firms may exact better prices. More importantly, these producer services will have the same labour market characteristics as described above that promote specialization and skills upgrading, thereby reinforcing agglomeration and the attractiveness of the financial centre as a place to conduct business. Hence, the y variable in our model, Fig. 1.3, is city-size and specialization. Accordingly, we assume that, on average, larger cities have, or have the capacity to pro-duce, a critical mass of financial and related intermediate services in sup-port of large-scale asset management, while also being at an advantage in the recruitment and retention of highly skilled and specialized knowledge work-ers. Note, however, that city-size and specialization do not necessarily increase together in the same direction. Although it is assumed that larger cities have the capacity to specialize and diversify into related services, that does not mean that larger cities are by default more specialized than smaller cities.

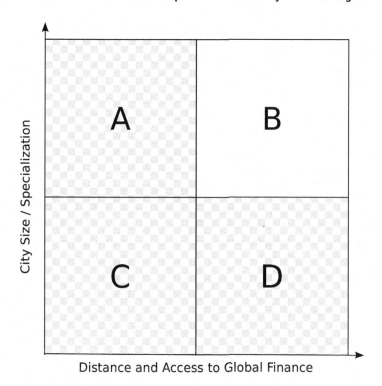

Fig. 1.3 The geography of finance

Acting to reinforce the hierarchical pattern and the concentration of financial activity in large IFCs in particular, is the risk management function of finance. For investors large and small, portfolio diversification is an important component of risk management. Risk-conscious investors thus tend to seek a range of financial products and geographic markets, which usually only large financial centres are able to provide, as a means of minimizing idiosyncratic risk, or rather the adverse consequences a loss on any one investment has on the portfolio as a whole. This process is reinforced by the issuers of securities and other financial services who are equally attracted to large financial centres by the demand generated by the large number of potential investors. At the same time, the geographical concentration of a large number of potential investors helps reduce liquidity risk, which is the speed and ability of an investor to convert an asset to cash, as they are brought together in the secondary market. In theory, deeper markets make it easier for firms and governments to raise capital while driving down the aggregate cost of capital.

We define our x variable, then, as distance and access to global finance. This variable is meant to capture the size and extent of the local market—assuming that for some places the local market is closer to, and/or part of, the global market, and therefore has better access to the lower transaction costs associated with accessing global markets. Like the *y* variable, distance and access do not necessarily increase and move in the same direction. A city, such as one in Australia or New Zealand, may be geographically very far from the core centres of global finance and even the core developed economies, but still cognitively, organizationally, socially and institutionally proximate.[6]

To clarify the logic of the model, quadrants A, C and D are tinted, because they represent frontier places. Quadrant B represents those places that are at the forefront in terms of market size and specialization, making them centres of global finance. Note that the model does not consider off-shore tax havens where little actual management of assets takes place. Furthermore, the model should not be seen as a replacement for more conventional city-rankings of financial services activity and interconnectedness.[7] Rather, the model should be seen as a conceptual typology that allows us to consider the organizational constraints facing frontier beneficiary institutions in managing and allocating capital. Specific examples are provided below to clarify the model.

Large Frontier Cities

Quadrant A identifies large cities on the periphery of global finance that may be regional financial centres, but are geographically distant or distant along some other dimension (e.g. cognitive distance). Likewise, local investment opportunities (i.e. the market) may be limited in size and scope and thus the opportunities for diversification. An example of such a city is Melbourne, which, as mentioned earlier, is a hub of investment management for the Australian superannuation industry. But, Melbourne is not the centre for Australian capital markets, which is Sydney. Melbourne is a relatively large city with over four million people, and given the size of the funds management industry there, the city is relatively developed in terms of the labour market for financial services, as is its cognitive and institutional proximity with the large Western IFCs. But, given Melbourne's geographic location, it is arguably more difficult to reproduce social and organizational proximity with actors in the major IFCs, thus complicating principal-agent relationships. The place of Melbourne also has to be considered in terms of the size and diversity of the Australian economy, which is insufficiently large to absorb the growth

---

[6] R. Boschma, *Proximity and innovation: a critical assessment*, 39 REGIONAL STUDIES (2005).
[7] See, for example, the bi-annual financial centre index produced by the commercial think-tank Z/Yen Group.

of compulsory pension savings. Going global is therefore a necessity for the Australian superannuation industry. Taking these factors together, Melbourne would sit in the lower right part of quadrant A.

Other cities in quadrant A could be the mainland Chinese cities Beijing and Shanghai. Although Shanghai is slightly larger than Beijing, its place as the leading financial centre in mainland China places it higher than and to the right of the latter. But, in both cases, and notwithstanding the size of the Chinese economy and its close (geographical and social) proximity with Hong Kong and Singapore, capital controls and the limited convertibility of the renminbi are, for example, regulatory-*cum*-institutional constraints limiting their proximity to global markets.[8]

Centres of Global Finance

In quadrant B are included the major international financial centres in terms of market size and specialization, as one normally sees in global rankings. In the top right of the quadrant would sit New York, London and Hong Kong. These three places house the headquarters of major international banks and investment services providers; they are the primary locations where large public companies are listed and traded; and they are the primary location investors come to access a wide variety of investment products. Elsewhere in quadrant B we can include Tokyo, given the size of the Japanese economy. Yet, Tokyo has receded as an international financial centre, which means it is far to the left of the above three, and arguably in the bottom left of quadrant B. Singapore, in contrast, would sit to the right of Tokyo, but it is normally not considered as significant as the three premier centres.

Small Cities on the Distant Frontier

In this quadrant sit those cities where the local labour and services market is highly limited in terms of specialization and where the transaction costs for accessing global financial markets are high because of either physical distance, or, for example, distance created by some other political-*cum*-institutional

---

[8] K. P. Y. Lai, *Differentiated markets: Shanghai, Beijing and Hong Kong in China's financial centre network*, 49 Urban Studies (2012).

constraint (e.g. political unrest).[9] These are also places where the size of the domestic economy is limited and where the local financial system remains underdeveloped. Here would be included cities in low-to-middle income economies, such as Botswana capital Gaborone or Dili, the capital of East Timor, both of which are home to commodity-based SWFs. Also included would be cities in central Asia such as Astana and Almaty in Khazakstan; or, cities close to major markets such as Tripoli in Libya and Algiers in Algeria, which although close in distance to the European market, are still likely to have constraints in terms of transactions costs and limited access locally to specialized services.

Small Cities on the Frontier

In quandrant D are those cities that by virtue of their location within larger markets have more access to global finance than cities in quadrant C. They are also more likely to be cognitively, organizationally, socially and institutionally proximate. Nonetheless, these cities may still have limits in terms of local labour markets, expertise and specialization. For example, Edmonton in Canada where AIMCo is based, would be included in quadrant D, given the size and scope of the North American market. But given the physical location of Edmonton and the size of the city, the scope of local expertise and specialization is limited. Edmonton is not the preferred working location for Canada's financial workers. This would mean it sits to the left of the quadrant.

Another example is the US city of Harrisburg, which is home to two large public pension funds. Although Harrisburg is closer to New York in terms of distance, it is a small city with limited recourse to financial expertise. We would also include a city such as Abu Dhabi in this quadrant, given that the Gulf states region has been growing in terms of its international links for all sorts of global economic activity and the proximity this brings, not least from the accumulation of commodity wealth and the spending power this provides governments in attracting such activity. Given the limited size of the local market, however, it would be placed on the far left; and given the limited scope and specialization of local financial services capabilities, it would sit in the bottom half of the quadrant.

---

[9] We are not suggesting that SWFs in low-income economies should access global finance. Addressing local capital scarcity is probably more beneficial for future generations than saving for them. There is a case, however, for commodity-based SWFs to hold low-risk securities to buffer against falling commodity prices.

In the top right corner of quadrant D would also be included cities such as Sacramento, home to two of the largest pension funds in the US, or the greater Randstad metropolitan area in the Netherlands, where most large Dutch pension funds are located. Both of these examples are places where financial expertise and services are more developed or where local opportunities (e.g. Silicon Valley venture capital in the case of Sacramento) are wider. Nonetheless, given their place outside a global financial centre—and the cognitive, organizational, and social distance this may entail—they still face agency issues when dealing with agents operating in global financial centres.

Conclusions

In the preface we suggested that the organizational innovation of large beneficiary institutions in places beyond the hinterlands of global financial centres, which we call frontier investors, represents a window of locational opportunity to remake the map of the investment management industry. In turn, we suggested that this innovation could undermine the dominance of large IFCs in the allocation of capital across time and space. Considering the significant size of these organizations in terms of assets under management, the scope for challenging the status quo to effect a realignment of the interests and outcomes between asset owners (and therefore beneficiaries) and the financial services industry is compelling, even if it is in the early stages.

There are still constraints that must be overcome if the status quo and the dominance of major IFCs and the service providers therein are to be altered significantly. We recognize that there is still insufficient critical mass to suggest a paradigmatic shift in the geography of finance away from its current form. This does not mean, however, that progress at the level of individual organizations is insignificant. The development of a new frontier of finance represents 'only a small series of fissures', like the development of other potentially progressive alternatives to the dominant power structures of global finance.[10]

It is therefore unsurprising that the global financial crisis, despite offering what looked like a window of opportunity to redefine and realign the social utility of the financial services industry, has not resulted in any major consequential change. In spite of mass protests and rhetorical gestures from the political classes, the crisis simply reinforced the consolidation and concentration of the industry that had been under way during the previous two

---

[10] J. Pollard and M. Samers, *Governing Islamic finance: territory, agency, and the making of cosmopolitan financial geographies*, 103 Annals of the Association of American Geographers, 723 (2013).

decades.[11] Commercial and investment banks in particular have become larger, not smaller. In the global geography of finance, the place of IFCs and the power of agents therein is unwavering.[12] While consolidation and concentration is due partly to political and regulatory decisions, it is also a function of economies of scale, scope and agglomeration. The enduring significance of these economic-geographical effects is borne out by the experience of the large beneficiary institutions we have engaged with, as the following chapters demonstrate. These frontier investors are developing ways of overcoming their organizational and geographical constraints. Unfortunately, it is uncertain if the movement will be adopted *en masse*, or whether their efforts are simply part of an ephemeral experiment that will eventually fail. Yet, in our view, if we are serious about making finance work for beneficiaries and the real economy, failure is not an option.

---

[11] E. Engelen et al., AFTER THE GREAT COMPLACENCE: FINANCIAL CRISIS AND THE POLITICS OF REFORM (Oxford University Press, 2011).

[12] D. Wójcik, THE GLOBAL STOCK MARKET: ISSUERS, INVESTORS, AND INTERMEDIARIES IN AN UNEVEN WORLD (Oxford University Press, 2011).

2

Unleashing Innovation Through Better Governance

A variety of macroeconomic factors have conspired against frontier investors globally. Pension funds in particular have been faced with the consequences of low interest rates, weaker growth prospects and ageing populations, leading to the ever-growing prospect that many will not be able to overcome their underfunded liabilities without doing something drastic. The threat of deep funding shortfalls is real. This precarious investment climate is making many plan sponsors (which are ultimately on the hook for the pension promises) uncomfortable, because the prospects of contribution increases or benefit cuts are not appealing.

Accordingly, many pension plan sponsors endorse a simple fix that will, if all goes well, make the above problems go away: the pension funds are to go out and make high returns, which are communicated to the pension fund through higher expected return targets. For this shortcut to full funding to be effective, however, pension funds will have to take on higher levels of risk. Indeed, it seems that for many pension funds, the only way they can align their return expectations with the policy mandate handed down by the sponsor is to be more aggressive and to invest in increasingly complex assets. This often means a swelling allocation to alternative asset managers, which, in turn, comes with higher fee regimes.

Going forward, more beneficiary institutions can be expected to search the world for new assets, sectors and geographies that will offer the risk exposures they require to return what they have promised to their stakeholders. And this change is not exclusive to pension funds. Many university endowments are being looked at to fund shortfalls in public research funding or to ease the

© The Editor(s) (if applicable) and The Author(s) 2016
J. Singh Bachher et al., *The New Frontier Investors*,
DOI 10.1057/978-1-137-50857-7_2

strain of increasing tuition. Taking greater risk seems to be the norm, but it also raises important questions:

- Should traditionally conservative beneficiary investors undertake these more aggressive strategies?
- Can they manage the organizational change necessary to cope with this shift in practice?
- Are these, often bureaucratic and complacent, organizations prepared to innovate in the ways required to be successful in these new riskier investments?

Again, the answers to these questions come down to the ability of an investor to innovate. For beneficiary institutions, becoming an innovative organization begins with focusing on the governance and management architecture: the rules and procedures that underpin performance and the beliefs that inform them. Even before the global financial crisis, some commentators argued that innovation in investment governance and management, especially over the long term, could create important gains.[1] The global financial crisis, which still lurks in our collective memory, has only strengthened the case for reform.

One would hope that the return of positive performance in financial markets has not brought back complacency. Booming markets can mask flaws in governance. But for many beneficiary institutions, no matter where they come from, governance is not something that is changed easily. National rules and regulations can be quite specific about what a pension fund or sovereign fund can and cannot do. Likewise, there may be few resources to make changes in a way that matters, at least in the short run. In reality, organizations are not likely to have as much freedom of action as proponents of better governance would hope. A single ready-made recipe for better governance is not so easily applied.

But just because there are constraints to how far governance and management can be changed, does this mean that the managers of beneficiary financial institutions and their boards should be complacent? Should they continue to follow the herd, as is commonplace? Most would probably agree that complacency is a dangerous thing, particularly in today's fast-moving global financial markets. The starting point to better governance is not about dwelling on one's constraints. Better governance and management starts by

---

[1] See K. P. Ambachtsheer, Pension revolution: a solution to the pensions crisis (John Wiley & Sons, 2007).

recognizing that it is an evolutionary process of mutual understanding and discovery.

Indeed, better governance is not something that appears overnight. Moreover, there should never be an end to better governance. Better governance, for beneficiary financial institutions large and small, comes from an awareness of how the fund is governed in the first instance, and constantly looking for ways to improve it over time. It is about embracing innovation. In that respect, thinking about governance becomes just as important as thinking about such decisions as asset allocation or external manager selection—'governance' is a code word for the resourcing of the investment organization. The resources required for success will inevitably evolve over time. Yet, knowing that all frontier investors are faced with individual circumstances, where does one start?

What sets frontier investors apart from generic investors on the peripheries of global finance is the intent among the former to run more of their own investment operations in place of relying exclusively on external asset managers. They are innovative organizations. They don't take the business of institutional investment and asset management as given. In this regard, frontier investors are attempting to reduce the agency problems present in the functional and spatial structure of the investment management industry, as outlined in the last chapter. While many frontier investors regard a functional and spatial reorganization of institutional investment as one way of realigning interests in the favour of beneficiaries (and potentially the recipients of capital), they also acknowledge the profound organizational and governance challenges associated with frontier finance. But taking on conventional practice is never easy.

As such, this chapter begins with the questions that all beneficiary financial institutions should be asking, if they want to take innovation seriously. These questions surround the mission and the beliefs of the organization and are ultimately about defining what the institution actually is and what is possible given existing resources and capabilities. We then move into a discussion of the role that investment beliefs can play in the implementation of innovative plans and the importance of investing in governance.

What's Your Mission?

No matter what the local constraints, beneficiary financial institutions usually have a singular purpose. Pension funds, for example, have a mandate to provide retirement income to beneficiaries. Few would disagree that this singular purpose should drive the governance and management of the organizations and, in addition, be reflected in a clear mission statement. Such clarity would put the beneficiaries at the forefront, helping to guide the setting of organizational and operational goals. Simply put, the long-term mission of these funds frame how elements of the investment process are resourced and supported in the context of unique constraints and available resources.

Some funds may, however, have more than one purpose. This is not necessarily a constraint. It could even be an advantage. But when the resources of any one organization are spread too thinly and committed to too many objectives, this can cause problems. Different objectives may require completely different investment styles. They may be subject to various time horizons. Simple administration may thus be completely different. Whatever the case, objectives and commitments, which are the basis of the fund's focus, need to be clearly recognized and accounted for. If conflicting or incongruent objectives cannot be reconciled, putting them in stark relief begins the conversation with the sponsor regarding whether a single fund or several funds are necessary.

What Do You Believe In?

In recent years, more beneficiary financial institutions have started to develop investment beliefs to help guide them over the long term. Textbook definitions of how financial markets are supposed to work have, we now know, limits. They are often based on abstract models that do not take into account the complexity of financial markets, the uncertainty of technological change, the expanding geographical scope of the investment universe and all the social and political complexity this entails, and the heterogeneity of financial market players. Hence, there is an awareness among long-term investors that they need to take a step back before any investment decisions are made and ask basic questions about the long-term prospects for the company, industry and market they are entering. This goes hand-in-hand with thinking about the mission of the fund and thus the place of the fund in the investment universe.

In our view, a clear set of investment beliefs provides a basis for strategic management of the investment portfolio. Such beliefs serve as a tool for making investment decisions by providing a context for investment management that will add value and a framework for assessing investment strategies. More importantly, clear investment beliefs help to avoid making changes in an ad-hoc way. Investment beliefs are about developing consistent views that allow you to avoid the pitfalls or even take advantage of the failings and misgivings of traditional theories of finance and investment. This is what many hedge funds are about: taking advantage of other investor's reliance on weak models.

What Is Your Comparative Advantage?

Just like the mission, investment beliefs should reflect the constraints and comparative advantages of an organization. If the managers of beneficiary financial institutions know their constraints, they should also know their comparative advantages. Knowing what can and cannot be done coupled with strong investment beliefs is the first step towards improving the investment process. For example, the comparative advantage that most beneficiary financial institutions share no matter the country of origin is a long time horizon, at least longer than many other investors. Better governance and management comes from recognizing this inherent characteristic, and drawing implications that are clear. For example, just as the compound rate of return is important for the portfolio, so is the compounded cost of managing the portfolio over time. As many beneficiary institutions still rely on external fund managers, better governance would suggest that a robust process of manager selection and cost management be in place.

In short, pension funds have some unique competitive advantages (e.g., time horizon) and challenges (e.g., human resources). Overcoming the challenges while maximizing the advantages is what better governance is all about. As such, pension funds should view their governance systems as long-term investments in their own right; this is not a cost but a profit centre for the fund! That principle we can all agree on.

Box 2.1: Translating Market Dominance into Competitive Advantage at APG

APG Group NV was formed in 2008 when the Dutch public sector pension plan ABP outsourced responsibility for the administration, management and provision of pension services to a wholly-owned subsidiary comprised of three entities: Algemene Pensioen (APG) NV, Cordares (51 per cent owned by APG Group) and Loyalis (90 per cent owned by APG Group). APG Pensions specialises in collective public sector pension schemes, while Cordares concentrates on collective private-sector pension schemes, especially in the housing and construction sectors, and Loyalis provides individual and insurance services to existing public and private sector scheme members.

APG Group provides the full range of services for the delivery of defined benefit pension benefits, including collectively agreed pensions, early retirement benefits, disability, sickness and death benefits. It also provides individual financial services. The population of the Netherlands is 16 million people; APG Group is responsible for 3.86 million participants where about 1 million participants receive a pension, 1.3 million are entitled to a deferred pension, and the balance are active pension plan participants. Over 400,000 participants have purchased insurance products of one form or another.

The Dutch pension system is based on social solidarity and the collective provision of supplementary workplace pension benefits aimed at a relatively high-income replacement rate upon retirement. Most Dutch employees are required to participate in a supplementary pension scheme, typically a multi-employer industry scheme. While the nature of pension benefits has evolved over time, becoming a hybrid defined benefit/defined contribution system, the investment of pension assets is intimately related to projected liabilities. APG group manages over $370 billion.

Competitive Advantage
APG Group dominates the Dutch pensions market and is one of the world's largest pension institutions. Being the result of a decision by ABP to outsource pension service provision to APG, most of its services, including investment management, are provided internally by the APG Group. In theory, it has three obvious competitive advantages when it comes to in-house asset management.

- *Economies of scale*: the volume of assets under management combined with the standardised nature of pension services provided to the vast majority of participants, allows APG group to claim cost advantages over its nearest Dutch pension fund (PGGM) and over large Dutch and European financial services companies. Economies of scale can translate into economies of scope, allowing APG Group to be the sole supplier for its clients.
- *Human capital*: being the dominant pension fund in the Dutch market and one of continental Europe's largest investment companies, APG Group has been able to recruit talented young professionals and experienced and knowledgeable mid-career financial professionals. While it has not been able to compete with London in terms of attraction of skilled workers, continuity of employment and relatively low career risk has given it certain advantages in retaining experienced and highly specialised professionals.
- *Investment horizon*: being a very large investment institution with a long-term investment horizon consistent with the nature of the pension benefit has allowed APG Group to deepen its expertise and maintain its commitment to a range of investment classes, despite the global financial crisis and the euro crisis. Compared with European banks and private financial institutions, APG Group is a patient investor.

How Do You Develop Investment Beliefs?

With a sense of purpose and a clear understanding of priorities in place, the organization can begin to reflect on its overarching beliefs about the world and the business of investing generally. A few simple questions offer considerable opportunity for differentiation among investors.[2] How do you view capital markets and how do you mobilize your views about capital markets in terms of organizational and ultimately investment strategies? After three decades of fairly regular crises, what is it that you believe about the business

---

[2] For a book-length treatment of investment beliefs see, Kees Koedijk and Alfred Slager, INVESTMENT BELIEFS: A POSITIVE APPROACH TO INSTITUTIONAL INVESTING (Palgrave Macmillan, 2011).

of investing and the behaviour of financial markets and agents? And, if you actually have cogent views on this subject and can articulate those views, how do they affect the way you deploy your capital? If you are frustrated with the tools at your disposal, what replaces these tools and their underlying assumptions? In other words, how do you develop a set of practical beliefs that can be mobilized in the real world?

In crafting investment beliefs that are useful, the focus should be on stating things one thinks are true about the markets that aren't obvious. Instead of saying "risk needs returns," it is more useful to consider and state things that are a less accepted and potentially controversial, such as, "investment decision-making is often irrational". If most would agree that risk needs returns, there is probably not consensus on whether investment decision-making is irrational. Some believe that markets are highly efficient, while others don't. And this is why no two institutions will have the same investment beliefs. If all investment beliefs were a recapping of Modern Portfolio Theory and the Capital Asset Pricing Model, everyone would say the same things about mean variance optimization, portfolio diversification and asset allocation.

This is not an argument for being contrarian. Taking a contrarian view can be highly profitable, but being contrarian can also be very dangerous. In our view, being contrarian is not a belief in and of itself. Rather, being contrarian is a product of the investment beliefs an investor holds. Put simply, your investment beliefs may drive contrarian behaviour just as much as they drive behaviour that appears rather conventional. So, how do you develop investment beliefs?

Limit Focus

Investment beliefs are unlikely to be completely independent of one another, and therefore must often be reconciled with one another to avoid both dissonance and unintended consequences if the beliefs are used as lenses through which to interpret and understand market outcomes and events, and decisions are based upon the beliefs.

That said, it seems extremely difficult to reconcile more than a few beliefs simultaneously in any sort of coherent way in all but the most specific situations. That is, investors may not be able to tell both cogent and robust stories about market function that incorporate more than a few beliefs at any one time. Therefore, it seems prudent that organizations focus on developing only a very limited number of 'core beliefs' and refining these at the highest level before examining further beliefs (possibly in more specific applications, such as with specific assets or geographies).

To be effective, investment beliefs must be developed to align with the objectives and orientations of the organization that holds them. The fact that an organization holds investment beliefs may not be sufficient to make its long-term belief systems coherent. Rather, it needs beliefs that are specifically designed to achieve the appropriate levels of coherence in the long-term. The following principles can help guide the setting of investment beliefs.

Alignment with Organizational Objectives

Having individuals within an organization with different understandings of what drives markets (or having understandings that clash with the 'organization's' position on such) pose a severe governance problem. All need not be of the same opinion on what is likely to happen, but there must be alignment of understandings of market processes (that is *how* things tend to happen). There can be disagreements on inputs, but the mechanisms driving price paths should largely be understood along similar (or the same) lines. The investment beliefs of individuals (if they have any) must be aligned with those of the organization (if it has any).

Understanding Influences

Knowing the forms of evidence that would cause one to reject or reaffirm a belief is important in the belief development process. Belief systems are better organized when it is understood what influences would alter the beliefs that comprise them (data, losses, academic proof, peers, etc.). Falsifiability is a good normative aim for beliefs (though difficult in practice).

Social Versus Internal Logic as Bases

There is strong evidence that holding certain beliefs individually is driven mostly by social factors, but that 'linking' beliefs in a coherent way requires some logical market 'story'. The importance of this 'story' grows with the number of beliefs being considered. Moreover, more stories start to exist with the number of beliefs under consideration. This finding provides insights of two forms. First, it supports the notion of focusing on development of a limited number of core beliefs. Second, it supplies a rationale that in developing investment beliefs, investors should be wary of (combinations of) beliefs upon which 'the market' is not in strong consensus ('zones of uncertainty').

These areas are likely to provide large returns if your beliefs are more coherent than those of the market and so your understanding is keener, but should be avoided if you do not think you are better than the market here or are risk-averse.

Mobilization

Beliefs are something that organizations should 'come back to' whenever they are either forming strategies/decisions or are facing new territory in terms of market developments, products and opportunities. They are, in a sense, necessary but not sufficient conditions for investment decisions, and therefore should be both the 'start' and 'end' points of any investment process. Further, investment beliefs can be regarded as a mirror through which organizations need to be self-critical and match their understandings of market functions/processes with their capabilities. That is, it is one thing to believe that perishable commodity markets may be inefficient, but quite another to know that your organization has the expertise (or can use out-sourced expertise) to exploit and operationalize that belief. The above logic was used in developing investment beliefs for the University of California Office of the Chief Investment Officer (see Box 2.2).

Box 2.2: Investment Beliefs for the Chief Investment Officer of the Regents

1. *We invest for the long term.* We focus on investments over 10 years and beyond where we can. This offers many more opportunities than those available to short- and intermediate-term investors.
2. *We invest in people.* The contributions of talented people drive the success for any investment organization. So we've made the recruitment and retention of exceptional staff a cornerstone of our strategy.
3. *We build a high-performing culture.* Every organization needs a clearly defined culture to make sure everyone is working towards the same ends and speaking the same language. Our culture is one of responsibility, accountability and high performance.
4. *We are all risk managers.* Our aim is simple: to earn the best risk-adjusted return that meets the objectives of our various portfolios. An effective risk management function enables leadership to delegate authority to the investment teams.
5. *We allocate wisely.* The key to investing, and the most important driver of performance, is asset allocation. To make effective investment decisions, and achieve the appropriate combination of risk and return, we have to

maintain a clear and balanced understanding of stakeholders' unique objections, time horizon, risk tolerances, liquidity and other constraints.

6. *Costs matter.* High quality advice comes at a cost. But we also believe fees and costs for external managers must be fully transparent. Plus, cost savings can be considered a risk-free return. We intend to capture every dollar of risk-free return we can.

7. *We diversify with care.* Diversification is invaluable, but it is not a cure-all. It allows us to spread risk and reduce the impact of any individual loss. But diversifying too broadly can draw you into assets and products you do not fully understand. We prefer a more focused portfolio of assets and risks we know extremely well.

8. *Sustainability affects investing.* Sustainability is a fundamental concern that we incorporate into our decision-making, particularly how it can improve investment performance. Sustainable businesses are often more rooted in communities and resilient, which means investing in them makes good business sense.

9. *We collaborate widely.* We are proud to be a part of the University of California, as well as the broader community of institutional investors. Through active collaboration, we aim to leverage the unique resources of the university.

10. *Innovation counts.* We must always be innovating and identifying new opportunities. There are advantages in thinking differently and partnering with peers that are willing to work with us on innovative projects. Collaboration is one of the most powerful drivers of innovation.

Investing in Governance

A big lesson from the subprime financial crisis was that many beneficiary investors did not understand the risks they had taken on with investments in mortgage-backed securities or associated derivative products. Some lessons have been learned since then, but it is reasonable to expect that many beneficiary investors, driven by excessively high return objectives, will once again venture into strategies and investment they do not understand.

Even if risk managers are looking for more risk, this is little consolation if the organization as a whole isn't prepared with the necessary resources and tools to communicate this information to the necessary systems or people. Skilled portfolio managers may be available, but are robust processes and protocols of decision-making coupled with the information processing tools that support those manager's judgments in place? In short, beneficiary investors considering new and risky strategies would be wise to consider whether they have the governance mechanisms necessary for effective supervision of the new and higher levels of risk.

For Gordon Clark and Roger Urwin, governance is a finite and measurable resource.[3] This led them to the concept of a governance budget, which refers to the budget available to support the tasks and activities necessary to operate effectively in global financial markets subject to risk and uncertainty. The financial logic of a governance budget is simple: if poor decisions are made because of inadequate understanding of investment risks and such insufficient organizational capability leads to lower returns and higher losses, then there are tangible, long-term financial gains to investing in more effective and more robust decision-making protocols and practices.

According to Clark and Urwin, a governance budget has three measurable ingredients:

- Amount of time that a fund can apply to a given investment problem.
- Level of expertise that can be called upon.
- Organizational commitment in terms of the responsive capabilities of the board (e.g. are decisions made in real-time or calendar time?).

We can look at each of these as being a scarce resource that can be drawn down as a fund engages in more innovative or risky behaviour. Each fund will have its own governance budget, which means that funds will have different organizational capabilities, different investment strategies and, most importantly, different risk budgets. Indeed, the essence of Clark and Urwin's thinking is that a fund's investment style and strategy should match its governance budget. This entails, furthermore, that a fund's risk budget should be closely related to, and synchronized with, its governance budget (Figs. 2.1 and 2.2).

Implementing the risky or new strategies that many funds are considering may require restructuring the internal governance of these funds. This can be a slow process, requiring considerable input from the fund's sponsors, and a willingness to switch authority from representative trustees or board members to people who are very sophisticated in investment matters. In the short run, then, rather than changing the governance to facilitate taking greater risks, it is perhaps wise to instead let existing governance capabilities drive and indeed constrain the level of risk-taking. In other words, beneficiary financial institutions should develop an investment strategy that is commensurate with their capabilities through the synchronization of the risk and governance budgets.

---

[3] G. L. Clark and R. C. Urwin, *Best-practice pension fund governance*, 9 JOURNAL OF ASSET MANAGEMENT (2008).

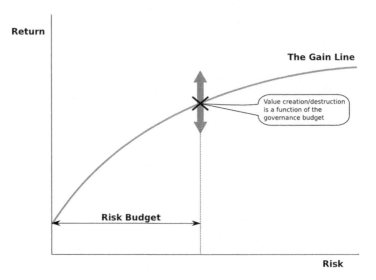

Fig. 2.1 Risk budget and governance budget synchronization

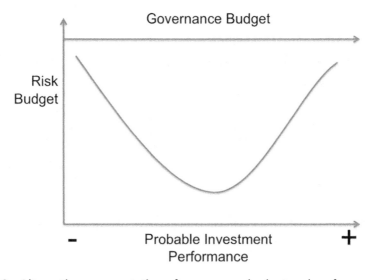

Fig. 2.2 Alternative representation of governance budget and performance

Conclusions

We can't recall ever seeing an institutional investor with a group focused exclusively on the research and development of innovative investment tools, methodologies or even technologies. There are 'special opportunities' groups and 'special situations' teams, and most investment organizations will usually have a strategy team that can do some applied research and development work. But none of these groups can be accurately characterized as 'research and development', because they do not really foster and exploit learning about innovation from a holistic perspective. This is odd.

An argument can be made that beneficiary institutions should add R&D to their organizational toolkits. This seems cogent for an industry that relies on informational advantages and knowledge, indeed it would institutionalize and formalize processes for creativity. Today, however, most beneficiary institutions are allergic to innovation. Most seem to prioritize efficiency and expediency at the expense of innovation. This is bad. Being a successful investor requires creativity and innovation.

The job of an institutional investor is to take money and turn it into more money. To achieve this, investors apply human resources and decision-making procedures to information with the hope of generating knowledge that can drive returns. That's all institutional investors really do. Seriously, that's it. Now, great investors combine talented people with effective procedures (governance) and unique information to create propriety knowledge and, thus, persistent outperformance. Research shows that knowledge is a resource as valuable as any other form of capital.[4] Indeed, investors are often judged according to their 'information ratio', because the secret of successful institutional investment is the development of knowledge and its management.

Yet 'knowledge' does not just happen. It is not something that can be outsourced (to, for example, pension consultants) because the best R&D and knowledge will be inevitably tailored to the circumstances of the investment organization. If a frontier investor is looking for alpha returns, it has to think hard about the kind of knowledge that it has the capacity to develop better than others. It needs to identify opportunities that do not fit in boxes and look for markets that are complex, inefficient and opaque. It should also focus on a subset of those markets in which it has an understanding advantage that it could use to identify endemic inefficiencies.

---

[4] R. E. Levitt, C.-M. A. Wang, P. S. Ho, and A. N. Javernick-Will, *A Contingency Theory of Organizational Strategies for Facilitating Knowledge Sharing in Engineering Organizations*, Global Projects Centre Working Papers *at* https://gpc.stanford.edu/sites/default/files/wp064_0.pdf

But to all of this unique knowledge, which can be a source of persistent and structural alpha to beneficiary institutions, one must apply innovation and creativity. And that, in turn, requires investors to develop mechanisms to think differently. Thinking differently begins with clarifying the mission of the fund, the investment beliefs, its comparative advantages and the capabilities available in terms of governance that guide and shape the execution of these elements. Such awareness, which is put into operation through a governance architecture that matches the capabilities of the fund, provides a basis for innovation. The best investors are those that accept financial markets as constantly changing ecosystems and, as a result, are trying to evolve dynamically through innovation to be able to reap returns. Good investment ideas do not last forever, which means there are significant rewards for spotting opportunities early and acting in an entrepreneurial manner quickly.

3

Unleashing Innovation Through People

The previous chapter stressed the importance of knowledge—of markets, of the organization and how the organization understands the markets and itself—in the investment management industry. At the centre of this knowledge development and management function rests the skills and competence of investment managers. If beneficiary financial institutions are to be successful, they must attract high calibre investment professionals and leaders. The reliance on human capital is compounded by the pervasive trend to invest in emerging markets and illiquid assets through in-house teams. However, frontier investors—such as public pensions or sovereign funds—face human resource constraints that generally stem from weak governance arrangements and the simple reality of geography; the relatively low pay and small pools of labour generally mean that successful human resources policies for these funds tend to require creativity and innovation.

This chapter highlights how certain public pension and sovereign funds are attracting the necessary human resources. The focus is on the recruitment of the organization's leaders, both current and future, within the investment departments. Although this addresses only a small segment of the fund's population, hiring talented investors is crucial to the success of any services-oriented business, especially in finance.[1] These principles and policies are illustrated through a case study of the Alberta Investment Management Corporation.

---

[1] David J. Teece, MANAGING INTELLECTUAL CAPITAL: ORGANIZATIONAL, STRATEGIC, AND POLICY DIMENSIONS (Oxford University Press, 2000).

© The Editor(s) (if applicable) and The Author(s) 2016
J. Singh Bachher et al., *The New Frontier Investors*,
DOI 10.1057/978-1-137-50857-7_3

Why Is it Hard to Find the Right People?

A report by CEM, a Canadian benchmarking company, shows that institutional investors, such as public pension funds, can achieve the same or better returns through in-house asset management for a fraction of the cost of outsourcing assets to external managers. These funds spend an average of 46.2 basis points on external management, compared with 8.1 basis points on internal investment capabilities.[2] Funds with internal management platforms perform better, driven largely by lower costs of internal management. In short, there are sound reasons for pension and sovereign funds (as well as their institutional cousins) to consider a policy of insourcing. And yet, the CEM report goes on to show that the successful funds at managing assets in-house have highly sophisticated and generous human resources offerings for employees. Indeed, these funds focus a great deal on attracting highly qualified individuals.

The question, then, is whether these public funds in frontier cities can attract the investment staff they will need to execute on these strategies. To do so, they will have to overcome the following constraints:

- *Public agency*: publicly sponsored funds investing in private markets have to find creative ways to fill 'public sector' jobs with individuals who can compete in and with the private sector.
- *Location*: while hiring skilled workers can be a challenge in any location, it is made more difficult by the fact that many public funds are located far from the world's financial hubs and, as such, pools of financial labour.
- *Alignment*: a challenge facing long-term investors is how to align the interests of new staff with the interests of the organization. Public pensions and sovereign funds have inter-generational time-horizons, while the funds' managers do not. This 'principal-agent problem' makes hiring and motivating people to act in the best interests of the fund difficult.
- *Direct investment*: funds that are moving assets in house need to hire 'investors' rather than 'allocators', but the former are harder to identify than the latter. Many institutional investors already have a pool of allocators who may have to be retrained or even let go. The direct investor will also have to hire the risk, operations and legal staff to manage the in-house processes.

---

[2] Jody MacIntosh and Tom Scheibelhut, *How large pension funds organize themselves: findings from a unique 19-fund survey*, 5 ROTMAN INTERNATIONAL JOURNAL OF PENSION MANAGEMENT (2012).

For every 'direct investor' the fund hires, it probably has to hire two back and middle office personnel to keep up with the workload.

- *Emerging markets*: if the fund is looking for exposure in emerging markets, it will need staff with local knowledge of these countries. Research shows that local knowledge and asymmetric information can lead to as much as 2 per cent per year in additional returns, which means this local knowledge is paramount.
- *Alternative assets*: if a pension or sovereign fund is looking to compete in alternative assets, skilled staff can become even more scarce and expensive than they already are in financial services generally.

In short, as funds on the frontiers of finance consider 'in-sourcing' or simply innovating within the long chain of intermediaries sitting between productive assets and pools of savings, their success will ultimately be a function of their ability to overcome the constraints above and attract the necessary people to succeed. But institutions are difficult to change, and it may take years for the public sector to converge towards private sector norms of human resources management. And this means that boards and managers of these frontier investors will have to become more creative.

The mistake most often made by beneficiary institutions is to underpay— sometimes dramatically—their people. The governing bodies that resource these funds will at times (erroneously) base the salaries of, say, sovereign fund staff, on government salaries instead of basing them off of market wages in finance. As the 2012 CEM study reveals, the top five highest earners at Canadian pension funds were paid $1.5 million, while the same people at US pension funds made only $372,000.[3] The fact that Canada has a world-class reputation for in-house management (and US funds do not) should not come as a surprise. The important thing to remember, however, is that the total costs (both internal and external) at Canadian funds were lower than the US funds and the returns were better!

Green, Grey, Grounded

Given the constraints cited above, public pension and sovereign funds face clear challenges in attracting investment talent. Yet, forward-looking and ambitious frontier investors have considerable success in hiring the *green*, the *grey* and the *grounded*:

---

[3] Idem.

- *The green*: public pension and sovereign funds are generally competitive in attracting early career individuals (i.e., the green). At this early stage (e.g., 0–5 years of experience), the disparity between public sector salaries and the private sector salaries are lowest. Moreover, the opportunities for career development at a public fund are (in many cases) superior to those in the private sector. As one investment chief told us, the sales pitch to his recruits begins, 'If you give me three years of your time, I'll give you 20 years of experience.' This tends to be a successful human resources strategy because many individuals will give up some current income to accelerate their career prospects and opportunities.
- *The grey*: public pension and sovereign funds are also competitive in hiring experienced individuals (i.e., the grey). Generally, these people have had careers in the private sector (e.g., 15–25 years' experience). They've made their money and are now interested in giving back or, depending on the circumstances at the fund, escaping the rat race. They also get to sidestep the fundraising cycle that so many private managers dread. They get a (relatively) stress free environment to 'practise their trade' through to the end of their careers. And they have the opportunity to act as mentors to younger employees (the green).
- *The grounded*: public pension and sovereign funds are also competitive at hiring people that are tied to the region (i.e., the grounded) because of family, identity or personal affinity. Indeed, many employees at public funds are there because they want to stay close to relatives, give back to their country, or just because they want to be close to some great skiing or fishing.

In summary, these are the types of people that seem most attracted to working at public funds. By implication, then, these funds are relatively less competitive at hiring the mid-career professionals who command high salaries in the private sector. That's not to say that there aren't some very talented mid-career folks. There are those that fall into the 'grounded' category and there are others that come for the same reasons as the 'grey' but are simply willing to leave the private sector earlier. Indeed, public funds will remain a second order option for the 'Wall Street' labour pool so long as these funds do not pay the market median for finance.[4] And very few funds have the governance arrangements that would see this pay level realized. As such, a dash of creativity and

---

[4] Keith Ambachtsheer, *How should pension funds pay their own people?*, 4 see idem at (2011); Robert Bertram and Barbara Zvan, *Pension funds and incentive compensation: a story based on the Ontario Teachers' Experience*, 2 ROTMAN INTERNATIONAL JOURNAL OF PENSION MANAGEMENT (2009).

innovation is required to compete. In our view, the three Gs of 'green, grey and grounded' represent a successful strategy for recruiting finance talent into public pension and sovereign funds today (see Box 3.1).

However, there is the potential for a different approach; one that makes no concessions to Wall Street managers or the private sector in terms of talent. Put simply, we think public funds should recognize how they differ from the mainstream and tailor their human resources strategies accordingly. In fact, they may get closer to achieving their objectives by seeking a different type of employee altogether.

Box 3.1: Attracting and Retaining Skilled Workers in Edmonton

The Alberta Investment Management Corporation (AIMCo) in Canada manages $70 billion on behalf of 26 public sector clients, including Alberta's pensions, endowments, and government funds.[5] It was launched in 2008 as a 'Crown corporation' to professionalize the management of provincial assets, which were previously managed by Alberta Finance and Enterprise. While the government remains the sole shareholder, AIMCo operates independently and has the overarching objective to build an effective asset manager with the capability to manage assets internally.

Since 2008, AIMCo has grown from 130 professionals to 300. The fund manages 80 per cent of its assets in-house, which means it has to hire highly sophisticated individuals. And yet, AIMCo is based in Edmonton, which can make recruitment a challenge. Even though the summers are beautiful and the geography is incredible, the winters are long. In addition, the city is not a global financial centre, which means there is no ready pool of investment managers to fill jobs. Moreover, the fund has to compete against the oil and gas industry for 'the green' employees (as well as operational workers). This makes AIMCo a useful case study for some of the human resource constraints discussed above.

On the issue of governance, AIMCo was the last of the big Canadian pension plans to be spun off from the Ministry of Finance into a Crown corporation. The fund followed the lead set by other Canadian funds, such as CPPIB and OTPP, by operating at arm's length to the government with a highly sophisticated board. The credibility (in terms of independence and business acumen) of the board has been key to attracting senior leaders to the organization. If a person is going to move their family to Edmonton, he or she will want confidence that the organization and its strategy have longevity. In addition, the board has put in place remuneration practices that are comparable with the private sector.

AIMCo focuses its recruiting on the individuals for whom the fund has an inherent competitive advantage in hiring. Like other funds, AIMCo has come to recognize that there are certain types of people that the fund is effective at recruiting, while there are other types of employees that are more challenging to recruit. Three types of people tend to fit AIMCo's competitive frame:

---

[5] The activities described in this box reflect the time when the first author was the Chief Operating Officer and Executive Vice President of Venture and Innovation at AIMCo.

- Early-career individuals who are 'rising stars' in their organizations. At the early stages of an individual's career, the disparity between AIMCo's salaries and the private sector salaries are low (or even in favour of AIMCo). Moreover, the opportunities for career development at AIMCo are far superior to those in the private sector, because young employees who demonstrate skill and are reliable tend to receive responsibilities far exceeding their peers in the private sector. In addition, these rising stars are given a 'bigger sandbox' to play in. To tap into this local talent, AIMCo sponsors local initiatives, such as a course at the University of Alberta and the Alberta Finance Institute in Calgary.
- AIMCo is also competitive at recruiting experienced employees at the later stages of their career. Many of these individuals are looking for an entrepreneurial challenge in a younger organization (i.e., less bureaucracy and more fun). These individuals tend to have had careers on Wall Street or in Toronto and are interested in spending a few years 'giving back'. They also tend to be the mentors for the rising stars, which is a crucial role for developing the organization's capabilities.
- AIMCo is also competitive at hiring people who have ties to the region through family, identity, affinity or geography. Indeed, many employees at AIMCo are there because they want to stay close to relatives, 'give back' to their province or simply live near some of the world's best skiing. AIMCo has grown adept at tapping into these local networks and finding talent therein.

By implication, then, AIMCo is less successful at hiring mid-career professionals who can earn high salaries in the private sector. However, that's not to say there aren't some of these mid-career people at AIMCo, but those at AIMCO in mid-career roles are often attracted by more than just money; it's often the platform (working for a $70 billion fund), the career acceleration (contacts, deals and experience); the mission (helping to provide pensions for the elderly), or the ability to avoid fundraising every 4 years (as private sector managers have to do) that drive the appeal of the job. And AIMCo does a good job of articulating these factors when recruiting mid-career people.

Tomorrow's Strategy: 'Moneyball'

Conventional finance wisdom has it that the highest paid investors are the best at their jobs. So, in theory, if an investment organization wants to have the best returns, it has to be willing to pay the highest salaries. Following this logic, a public pension or sovereign fund can never really hope to compete in the financial marketplace because of resource constraints, which is why these funds should outsource their investment mandates to the highly paid professionals in the private sector. Is this right? We think not. In fact, we do not equate the compensation of Wall Street asset managers with their ability to generate long-term returns at a public pension or sovereign fund.

Consider the telling case study of the baseball team the Oakland A's, as high-lighted in Michael Lewis's book *Moneyball*.[6] At the time, the prevailing theory in baseball was that the teams with the highest paid players would inevitably have the most wins. However, something strange began happening when the team with the lowest payroll, the Oakland A's, began consistently beating the teams with the highest payrolls. In fact, the A's fielded a winning team with a payroll that was a quarter of the highest paid teams. This raised the question as to how a resource-starved team could consistently beat teams with 'better players'.

The team's success was driven by its willingness to revisit the fundamentals of the game to work out what actually makes a winning baseball team. With this information in hand, the management set out to hire players who could maximize the team's capacity in those domains that had the highest correla-tions with winning. Put simply, the team gave up on the 'conventional wisdom' of baseball and re-conceptualized the characteristics of a winning team. And by revisiting the foundations of baseball, the team found a set of *cost-effective* ingredients that could replicate the *costly* ingredients used by other teams.

The story has parallels in the world of beneficiary financial institutions and the 'game' of finance. These resource-constrained investors need to attract people who can compete in and with the private sector but at a fraction of the cost. To accomplish this, they, too, need to re-examine the very nature of finance and investment. Moreover, they will need to re-examine the con-straints and comparative advantages they bring to the table. These are the ingredients they have at their disposal. And with these ingredients to hand, the funds can identify the types of individuals who can add the most value for the organization over the long-term.

In the most generic terms, a beneficiary financial institution's objective is to generate financial returns over the long-term. These funds are thus (in theory) unconstrained, long-term investors. They should behave in a different manner from short-term, private sector managers. These long-term investors should thus see the 'game' they're playing as one where 'the winners' generate sustain-able economic growth and value through investments in a (reasonably) diversi-fied portfolio of assets. In our view, this requires thinking about real assets and companies rather than focusing on abstract financial products and concepts.

All this is to say that the game a long-term investor plays is different from the game short-term investors play, which means that a different type of employee may be 'the ideal type' for the former than for the latter. For example, public funds may want to hire people who can think in concrete terms about creating

---

[6] Michael Lewis, MONEYBALL: THE ART OF WINNING AN UNFAIR GAME (W. W. Norton, 2003).

businesses and generating value. Consider, as a tangible example, the skill set required for assessing a farmland investment in the manner outlined by long-term pension investor TIAA-CREF:

> In every acquisition, our agricultural investment team considers farm-specific investment criteria. These factors take into account regional and microclimate factors, including weather variability and soil types; the strength of local infra-structure and tenant markets; water availability and sustainability; crop returns; environmental and social impacts; the potential for future operational growth; and capital gains. Our investment decision-making is also based on crop type... .[7]

There are no financial abstractions in making such investment decisions. The investor is seeking insight into how this asset will develop and grow (literally) for decades. We think this is a useful way for long-term investors to approach investments of all kinds.

So let's reconsider the human resources question again: what type of person would be better suited to making farmland investment? Put another way, what game is the investor playing above and is it the same game that the highest paid hedge fund managers are playing in New York and London? The answer is almost certainly No. Let's also pose the question as to whether an investment professional with experience of structuring and assessing various financial products and their risks would be the appropriate choice for managing a portfolio of farmland investments over time? Or, rather, would an agricultural professional with experience of developing farming businesses be the better option? If we were planning to hold the asset for 30 years, we'd choose the latter.

In short, long-term investors are focused on creating lasting value (rather than just taxing market inefficiencies, which seems to be the focus of short-term investors these days). Long-term investors build businesses, buildings, bridges and, yes, they even plant beans. They invest directly to avoid the distortionary (short-term) influence of intermediation. They look for ways to remove unnecessary abstractions to evaluate the long-term growth prospects for a given asset. In our view, then, public funds should not be trying to tempt employees away from Wall Street; they should be looking for people with a slightly different make-up who can drive sustainable growth for decades to come.

With this in mind, we'd rather hire an army of project managers with little knowledge of finance than hire an army of investment professionals with little

---

[7]TIAA-CREF (2012). 'How We Invest: Brazil Farmland: Emerging Market, Growing Opportunity.' www.tiaa-cref.org/public/about/asset-management/innovation-stories/brazil-farmland. Accessed 15 October, 2015.

project management experience—especially since all public pension and sovereign funds will have a senior investment professional (e.g., the chief investment officer) who will have to bless any investment decisions anyway. Why project managers? Because they are team players (most of what they do is coordinate and delegate). They are disciplined and rigorous about getting things done. They can navigate bureaucracies, while internalizing and integrating innovative practices. And, finally, they have a high tolerance for ambiguity. This is the practical reality of life inside a sovereign fund, and these are the individuals that we think would make up a winning team for less money.

Conclusions

Because institutional investment is a talent intensive industry, public pension funds and sovereign wealth funds have to attract high calibre investment professionals and leaders to be successful. The funds' reliance on human capital tends to be compounded by the pervasive trend to invest in emerging markets and illiquid assets through in-house teams.

However, public funds—like many institutional investors—face human resource constraints that generally stem from weak governance arrangements and the simple reality of geography; the low pay and small pools of labour generally mean that human resources policies for these funds tend to require creativity and innovation. Today's public funds are thus adopting human resources strategies that focus on segments of the labour market where they are competitive.

In general, funds are seeking three types of people. First, people who are early in their careers and want experience (the green); second, late career employees who want a change of pace from Toronto, the City of London or Wall Street (the grey); and people tied to the region because of family, identity, affinity or geography (the grounded). However, while this approach offers public funds the ability to get the talent they need, the three Gs only offer a short-term solution.

Tomorrow's public funds will want to re-consider the very nature of finance and investment and the objectives of their organizations. In our view, long-term investors such as public pension and sovereign funds should be focused on generating lasting value, creating businesses, buildings, bridges and even planting beans. And the people they hire to achieve these goals should be expert at these tasks. In other words, public funds will have to re-conceptualize the types of people that best align with the fund's objectives; this is 'moneyball' finance.

4

Unleashing Innovation Through Collaboration

Around the world's financial markets, the prudent person rule is seen time and time again as the guiding light for trustees, directors and fiduciaries of beneficiary investment organizations. In the US, for example, the rule says that fiduciaries must act solely in the interest of beneficiaries, 'with the case, skill, prudence and diligence under the circumstances then prevailing that a prudent man acting in a like capacity and familiar with such matters would use in the conduct of an enterprise of a like character with like aims'.[1]

This sounds sensible, but it has some terrible consequences. Specifically, the problem with prudent-person rules is the perverse incentive they create for beneficiary institutions to avoid innovation and hold on to convention. Research shows that these rules push investment organizations to hug benchmarks and avoid doing anything that would make them stand out from the crowd. As Russell Galer, a pensions policy expert, puts it, 'to find out what ordinary prudent persons are doing, one might, quite naturally, look at peer average or relevant index as a benchmark. Indeed, trustees are likely to find themselves in breach of their fiduciary obligations—and potentially legally liable—if their plan's investment performance (or the performance of any investment manager that they have engaged on behalf of the plan or fund) is consistently below average and they have taken no steps to address the situation.'[2] Oxford academic Gordon Clark suggests that 'instead of looking forward and being part of a process whereby community norms and conventions adapt to a changing

---

[1] See, 29 US Code section 1104, fiduciary duties.

[2] R. Galer, *Prudent person rule standard for the investment of pension fund assets*, OECD FINANCIAL MARKET TRENDS (2002).

environment, trustees may seek refuge in the past where certainty prevails, albeit at the cost of reinforcing convention.'[3]

Consider the example that the prudent person rule makes an explicit case for diversification, 'so as to minimize the risk of large losses'. What about the notion that the more diversified you become, the less you truly understand the risks in your portfolio? Investors are nothing more than risk managers, so shouldn't they be allowed—and sometimes encouraged—to manage risk in concentrated pools or in new ways? Let's not get into the fact that a broadly diversified portfolio of assets you barely understand is more risky than a concentrated portfolio of assets you know well and have a high conviction in. Let's instead just consider doing things differently from the crowd so as to get more return per unit of risk.

One of the governing principles of beneficiary institutions—the very principle meant to protect them—is partly to blame for their inability to innovate and professionalize, which renders them vulnerable to powerful interests in the finance industry—and facilitates these intermediaries in extracting rents that far exceed the value created by the finance ecosystem. But, it's not all bad news, there is actually a work-around that allows the truly innovative beneficiary investor to move beyond antiquated notions of prudence and fiduciary duty: peer-to-peer collaboration.

The Benefits and Challenges of Collaboration

It seems clear that long-term institutional investors, such as public pension and sovereign funds, could benefit from working together. They can share local knowledge and asymmetric information as well as pool skill-sets, deal pipelines and networks. Moreover, the fact that one institution can convince others to work together on a creative project allows all of them to claim prudence under the prudent person rule. In general, however, the benefits of peer-to-peer collaboration come in six types:

* *Higher returns*: communities of like-minded, frontier investors can, in theory, leverage one another's local advantages on a global basis, which can help bolster returns.[4] For example, research shows that tapping into local knowledge can translate into as much as 2 per cent in additional returns a year.[5]

---

[3] Gordon L. Clark, *Fiduciary Duty, Statute, and Pension Fund Governance: The Search for a Shared Conception of Sustainable Investment* SSRN *at* http://ssrn.com/abstract=1945257

[4] Meric S. Gertler, *Tacit knowledge and the economic geography of context, or the undefinable tacitness of being (there)*, 3 Journal of Economic Geography (2003).

[5] Joshua D. Coval & Tobias J. Moskowitz, *The geography of investment: informed trading and asset prices*, 109 Journal of Political Economy (2001).

- *Saving costs*: pooling resources through collaboration and co-investment can be a useful way of sharing costs, such as due diligence, human capital, and research.
- *Deal flow*: co-investment platforms offer access to deals that some funds would otherwise find difficult to source and validate.
- *Diversification*: co-investments offer investors the benefits of direct investing with the diversification of holding a broader portfolio of assets.
- *Governance rights*: co-investing allows investors to bypass traditional intermediaries and maintain complete control over investments.
- *Headline risk*: working together can minimize headline risk and mitigate political risk.

The benefits of collaboration and co-investing are clear. So, why aren't there more examples of collaboration and co-investment among institutional investors? No doubt there have been some ad-hoc club deals, and institutions often formalize collaboration with private managers through co-investment rights. But few examples of formal peer-to-peer collaboration exist.[6] Over the past decade, numerous attempts have been made to launch co-investment platforms, and many have failed to achieve their original objectives. Why?

Generally, there are factors that make this sort of peer-to-peer collaboration difficult. These factors fall into five categories:

- *Structure*: can you actually set up a formal mechanism for sharing deals that is agreeable to all parties (e.g., loose or formal; discretion or non-discretionary)?
- *People*: can you persuade non-executive staff to coordinate? Can the investors hire the people they require to be good partners (e.g., experienced or novice; seconded staff or external recruits)?
- *Governance*: how do you get buy-in from each fund's leadership for the requirements to run the collaborative endeavour when there may be barriers from public bureaucracy, constrained resources or an allergy to innovation?
- *Institutional*: can an investor find like-minded parties with the same investment beliefs, culture and philosophy? Can large institutional investors get along with other large institutional investors? What happens when the leadership changes at one of the participating funds?
- *Regulation*: are funds going to have to challenge the in-house lawyers to get this off the ground when it comes to fiduciary duty and compliance?

---

[6] However, as Monk and Sharma (2015) have highlighted, more examples are emerging.

These are serious challenges. And, as a result, many senior executives at public pensions and sovereign funds have become cynical and sceptical about co-investment platforms that seek to bring peers together around an investment proposition or philosophy. But, given the benefits, we believe the institutional investment community should persevere and find a way to work together.

To consider how the community of institutional investors and beneficial institutions can move forward in terms of collaboration and co-investment, the next section offers an in-depth case study of an investor grouping that was able to collaborate and invest through a bespoke vehicle tailored to meet their needs: the Cleantech Syndicate. Drawing on the insights from this case, we then sketch out some paths forward for co-investment vehicles more generally.

The Cleantech Syndicate

At the time of the case study (circa 2011–2012), the Cleantech Syndicate was a group comprised of 14 family offices, representing about $40 billion in capital. Conceived of in June 2010 by Black Coral Capital (a family office) and McNally Capital (an administrator), the syndicate's stated mission was to assemble a select group of family offices to 'pool expertise, resources and capital to invest directly in clean technology and alternative energy companies'. It was a virtual private equity shop with all aspects of the value chain and investment stages covered, with family offices offering staff to act as 'partners'. There were 30 team members dedicated to the syndicate, including 17 'institutional quality' clean technology investment professionals. The group had $1.5 billion to deploy into this asset class, which made the syndicate among the world's largest players in this niche market. The over-arching objective of the syndicate was simple: *transactions*. In 2011, the period in which the research was conducted, there were about 10 deals closed, with three of those deals having several families represented.

Motivation

The families that came together to form the syndicate were all institutional investors with professional investors working within their organizations. These investors came to realize that the external fund manager model simply didn't work for clean technology. The performance of the funds did not justify the fees and the time horizon of the investments was too short, which left the families looking around for options. At a certain point, they started investing directly, and the syndicate offered a path towards direct investing that was realistic given their resource constraints. The syndicate solved several problems for its members:

- *Deal flow*: the syndicate was a very large investor in this niche market. Almost every deal in North America (and the world) comes through the inboxes of either the syndicate administrator or one of the families. For example, syndicate members saw, in rough numbers, 1500 deals in 2010 and 2011.
- *Scale*: cleantech investments require a significant commitment of capital over the long term to succeed. Raising this capital can be a challenge, but working together in the syndicate makes this much easier.
- *Expertise*: syndicate members have, in most cases, already built successful businesses in the marketplace, which means they offer considerable insights into different segments of the industry. The members exchange investment ideas and assist on due diligence and vetting as well as offer advice on portfolio companies.
- *Post-close*: syndicate members are intent on creating value beyond the transaction. Members have indicated that the group has become invaluable for identifying potential customers or suppliers for portfolio companies. In short, the long-term goal of the syndicate is to create value beyond the deal; in the words of one member, 'That's the magic dust.'
- *Due diligence*: one important function the syndicate plays is providing advice that prevents members from doing a 'bad' deal. This is hard to quantify but valuable.
- *Costs*: access to third-party industry reports and attendance at cleantech conferences become time and cost efficient when the benefits are spread across a larger group.
- *Relationships*: the syndicate offers family offices a unique platform for developing relationships among the members *and* external partners. The syndicate can serve as an outward-facing organization that offers external partners an easy point of access through which to seek (or bring) opportunities.

In short, the syndicate is all about institutions coming together to collaborate (e.g., sharing content, knowledge and deal flow) and co-investment (e.g., sharing capital and risk).

Structure

The syndicate was not set up like a private equity fund. The group operates based on loose principles and policies, with discipline coming from mutual respect and trust (and, it seems, the threat of embarrassment and expulsion). Most of the family offices did not even have non-disclosure agreements in place. Instead, there was a sense that the participants wanted to work together for decades, so they would not do anything silly in the short term that could prevent that. Additionally, members were carefully screened to ensure fit. And the approval process was often lengthy, because there was a variety of pre-requisites. For example, some of the basics included setting a certain level of assets under management in the sector and a full-time employee dedicated to doing direct investments in the space. All potential members were asked to complete a detailed new member survey that drilled down into the family's cleantech portfolio. Also, new members had to be sponsored by existing members, and the total membership was capped to prevent the group getting too big. Beyond those criteria, there also had to be a willingness to share knowledge and information as well as having some unique access to deal flow.

Responsibilities

Syndicate members had several responsibilities. They were expected to recommend prospective investment opportunities as well as lead the investment process for select opportunities. They might be asked to bring in non-syndicate co-investors when necessary. A member would also act as a resource for other members, perhaps even assisting with due diligence. For this to function, the member has to be present (on calls and at meetings). The ethos of the organization was to develop trust through engagement and responsiveness (i.e., being a good citizen of the syndicate). Members were expected to return each other's phone calls and respond to emails in a prompt and courteous manner *at a minimum*. And those members that did not play by the rules, were politely asked to quit the group. Interestingly, the fifth member to join the syndicate was 'asked' to leave, which had a motivating effect on the remaining members.

Investments

The family offices in the syndicate were all professional institutional investors. They all had the internal capability to prosecute deals on their own. All were direct investors in cleantech, which is why they were motivated to join the syndicate in the first place. Accordingly, the families can all lead deals. So when a deal came in of value, one family would tend to lead the deal with one or two other families helping with various aspects of the diligence. The syndicate seemed to fill gaps in the members' internal capabilities when it came to doing a direct investment.

Implementation

The successful functioning of the syndicate appeared to be due to the following factors:

- *Intermediation*: an administrator driving the day-to-day sharing of deals and information: Chicago-based McNally Capital.[7] This administrator was crucial to the functioning of the syndicate, because everyone was too busy to prioritize this group over their own business. McNally spend a lot of time thinking about what the members were interested in and working on. Deals were shuffled back and forth and McNally flagged areas where one member might help another. McNally knew the holdings of all the members' cleantech portfolios, which allowed it to identify opportunities to leverage the collective knowledge of the group. *The lesson of this is to assign an independent party to administer the syndicate—the goal is to provide the appropriate structure and process facilitation.*
- *Enforcement*: the syndicate diligently enforced any rules or guidelines that were accepted by the group. The intermediary thus plays the role of 'policeman' (even if the 'judge' may be the syndicate itself). *So, the intermediary also has to act as policeman, which makes it necessary to have an objective third party playing this part.*
- *Mandate*: the syndicate set the scope of the mandate very clearly. In its view, the organization would never work if the group was industry agnostic. *Have a clearly defined mission based on actions rather than concepts.*
- *Membership*: to ensure success, the syndicate spent a great deal of time determining the types of members it would accept. This has been crucial for keeping the momentum going. *It is important to take the time to determine what an 'ideal member' is for a given group.*

---

[7] www.mcnallycapital.com

- *Commitment*: nobody gets into the group without real commitment, and nobody stays in the syndicate without real commitment. This commitment can be quantified, by factors such as a full-time employee in the industry, fees and capital allocations, as well as being perceived as supportive by other members. *When adding members, consider equally their suitability with the group's mission and their ability and desire to be active participants. Do not underestimate the importance of creating good group chemistry.*

- *Momentum*: the syndicate has so much momentum that members would be embarrassed if they were not living up to their peers' expectations. *Obtain a critical mass that drives the organization forward; empower champions early and often.*

- *People*: the syndicate has the right people in the room when it comes to co-investing; it's all well and good to have high-level buy-in, but getting the buy-in of staff is often a challenge. At the syndicate, staff drives the process (because their incentives are properly aligned). *It's not enough to get senior leaders to buy in. Staff and lawyers have to be intimately involved.*

- *Competition*: membership of the syndicate was built to maximize coverage and knowledge areas and to minimize direct competition among families for deals. They try to have close enough alignment to have synergies, but not so close as to view each other as competitors. *Each member of the syndicate should bring a skill, know-how or network that complements that of the broader group.*

- *Sharing*: membership of any transaction-oriented organization has to be open to sharing *valuable* content, contacts and, especially, deals. For example, syndicate members are expected to make room on their good deals for other members. So if a member has a $5 million deal, the sourcing family might take $3 million and leave $2 million for other members (rather than taking the whole $5 million) because they want to support the syndicate (and tap into the expertise of the other family offices). *Members have to be willing to give of themselves in the short-term to ensure the long-term success of the syndicate.*

- *Origins*: the syndicate could not have come about without a handful of families acting as early champions for the concept. This generated enough momentum to kick-start the organization. Had an intermediary tried to start the syndicate from scratch, there would have been too much suspicion and fear of misalignment for any of the families to embrace the concept. *It is crucial to have institutional investors driving the launch of the group to ensure legitimacy and alignment of interests.*

As these implementation lessons demonstrate, the Cleantech Syndicate thought long and hard about co-investment challenges and how to overcome them. They are to be commended for their perseverance in this regard.[8]

A Path Forward

The syndicate example offers useful lessons for institutional investors considering co-investment vehicles. Obviously, family offices differ from a sovereign fund or a pension fund, but they are sufficiently similar to draw useful insights (e.g., all are long-term institutional investors; all prefer direct investments; and all are constrained by resources). Moreover, their motivations for launching the syndicate (e.g., deal flow, scale, expertise, diligence and costs) match up with many of the reasons for large institutional investors launching co-investment vehicles. In this section, then, we draw lessons from the Cleantech syndicate. In particular, it will be useful to draw on the implementation framework from above:

- *Intermediation*: the success of any co-investment initiative will require a pro-active administrator.
- *Enforcement*: the intermediary will play the role of policeman, ensuring that members are abiding by rules and being good citizens.
- *Mandate*: to be successful, the co-investment initiative has to have a clearly defined mandate and theme. This will ensure that only 'quality' deals are brought to the group. (It also makes it easier to determine which deals are appropriate for the group.) These groups should seek to define as much as is possible and feasible (such as size, industry and geography).
- *Membership*: not every co-investment platform is going to be appropriate for every institutional investor. Investors must be methodical in determining which funds are brought into which groups, because these vehicles will only work when investors are truly like-minded. Funds must not underestimate the importance of 'good chemistry' in the success of any initiatives.
- *Commitment*: members of a co-investment group must demonstrate some level of tangible commitment to the group and its theme (full-time employees, capital).
- *Momentum*: the group has to establish a critical mass before launch.

---

[8] Ward McNally of McNally Capital jokes that the secret of the syndicate was '…the track marks on my back from getting run over so many times'.

- *People*: the success of any collaborative initiative will be a function of the incentives of the people working within the group. The staff doing the heavy lifting to make these groups work should have performance pay tied to the objectives of the collaborative initiative.
- *Competition*: members must bring differing skillsets and networks to create synergy rather than competition.
- *Sharing*: members have to be willing to give up some short-term gains to ensure the long-term success of a syndicate.
- *Origins*: institutional investors driving the launch of any platform or vehicle should have aligned interests to ensure legitimacy.

Setting Up Co-investment Vehicles and Platforms

With the above principles for success in hand, the pressing question, then, is how co-investment vehicles and platforms should be structured. Based on our experience, there are three options available to institutional investors: an alliance, a syndicate, and a seed.

The Alliance

This group is characterized by a loose affiliation of like-minded investors around an investment theme to share deals and resources. The objective is to institutionalize collaboration and co-investment, offering direct investors the opportunity to tap into a network without entering into legal agreements (e.g., seed) or dealing with the bureaucracy of external administration and intermediation (e.g., syndicate). Deal flow will be generated by alliance members through existing channels and then reconciled *by the members' own teams* for presentation to the alliance. Using the implementation framework described above, here is the way an alliance could be set up:

- *Intermediation*: members will internalize this function. Perhaps they could take leadership roles in turns.
- *Enforcement*: the group will have to play the role of policeman and judge.
- *Mandate*: the alliance will refine the investment theme along industry, size and asset class so as to ensure only 'quality' deals are presented.
- *Membership*: a questionnaire or survey can be used to assess suitability.
- *Commitment*: members will dedicate capital (perhaps formally or through setting funds aside) and staff (either on secondment or as a full-time employees working on alliance matters exclusively).

- *Momentum*: this will have to be member-driven.
- *People*: staff will have to be seconded directly from members.
- *Competition*: members should be selected carefully.
- *Sharing*: this will have to be member-driven.
- *Origins*: because the alliance will be investor-run, it will be fully aligned.

Questions to consider: How do you prevent free riding? How to you police membership? How do you ensure momentum?

The Syndicate

This type of group is characterized by a formal affiliation of like-minded investors around an investment theme to share deals and resources. Syndicate members make a formal agreement through a credible and objective intermediary that will coordinate the sharing of deals and knowledge. This is the model that was adopted by the Cleantech Syndicate. Using the implementation framework described above, here is the way a syndicate could be set up:

- *Intermediation*: a formal administrator is appointed to act as the go-between.
- *Enforcement*: the administrator will play the role of policeman and judge.
- *Mandate*: the syndicate will refine the investment theme along industry, size and asset class so as to ensure only 'quality' deals are presented.
- *Membership*: a questionnaire or survey can be used to assess suitability.
- *Commitment*: members will dedicate capital and contribute resources to staff the organization (i.e., pay the administrator).
- *Momentum*: this will be driven by the members but encouraged by the administrator.
- *People*: members will second internal staff and pay for an administrator to round out any gaps in the internal capabilities of members.
- *Competition*: members should be selected carefully.
- *Sharing*: this will be driven by members and facilitated by the administrator.
- *Origins*: the syndicate will be sponsored by the investors, which should ensure alignment over the long term.

Questions to consider: Can public investors find the resources to pay for an administrator?

The Seed

This group is characterized by a formal legal structure, such as a general partnership (GP) or limited liability partnership (LLP), that brings together likeminded investors around an asset manager set up from scratch and staffed by seasoned investors. The objective of seeding a new asset manager is to maximize the alignment of interests (and minimize fees) between the asset owners and the asset managers by extracting concessions from the asset manager upon launch of the vehicle. A seeded vehicle is structured by the limited partners (LPs) for their own exclusive benefit (e.g., low fees, control and no fund raising). This structure can be applied to a variety of asset classes and industries; the key is agreeing to a refined mandate to attract sufficient interest.

Let's apply the collaboration framework to this model:

- *Intermediation*: seed members will delegate authority to an intermediary (unless the LPs want to be part of the GP as well, which is reasonable).
- *Enforcement*: this becomes less of an issue because the commitment of members is secured.
- *Mandate*: the seed will have a refined investment theme, as this will be necessary for hiring the investment team.
- *Membership*: a questionnaire or survey can be used to assess suitability, but this is less relevant for seeds.
- *Commitment*: seed members will commit capital to the new vehicle.
- *Momentum*: the group's new management team will drive this.
- *People*: the decision to seed a vehicle is almost always a function of the talent available in the marketplace.
- *Competition*: this depends on where deals are being sourced.
- *Sharing*: this is not an issue (though it does depend on where deals are being sourced).
- *Origins*: the seed will be launched by the investors, which should ensure alignment over the short- to medium-term. (However, past cases do show alignment deteriorating over time.)

Questions to consider: Can the funds seeding the vehicle achieve the level of control they want over the assets in the fund? What happens over the long term?

The Choice

The choice of platform—alliance, syndicate or seed—will be a function of the funds populating the vehicle and their constraints and requirements.

Ultimately, the choice will reflect the problems faced by the funds participating. Indeed, all the participating funds should be asking what their problems are with the current offerings in the market for financial services. Is it duration, alignment, sourcing, control, resources, knowledge, or diligence? Or is it all of these? The answers to these questions will drive the vehicle selected for the innovative strategy and approach. For example, if a fund has no interest in control of the underlying assets that are being invested in—or governance rights of any kind—then seeding a new asset manager could be perfect. However, if a fund wants to be able to exert direct influence over assets, the syndicate or alliance approach may be more appropriate. Funds will also have to consider the resources they have available, as different vehicles will require appropriate resourcing. An alliance or syndicate will probably put a burden on the fund's internal costs, while the seed path tends to fall into the 'fee' line of the budget (which, in many cases, isn't as closely vetted by boards or policymakers as internal costs). The seed path may be useful for breaking out from internal resourcing constraints.

Conclusions

In the wake of the global financial crisis, institutional investors are rethinking the way they access markets. Are they going to continue relying only on external managers? Or are they going to in-source a portion of their investment operations and rely on peers to fill gaps in their abilities? Or are they going to do something different, such as seeding third-party managers? All of these options are being viewed in light of the high fees and seemingly misaligned interests of the current third-party fund model. In short, the ways in which large investors deploy assets are being remade.

Generating alpha is about knowing something that others don't. But it is much more than this. We like to think that markets are democratic and open to everyone. However, so many of the biggest players (e.g. Yale University's investment office, venture capital firms and Goldman Sachs) capture alpha because they have privileged access, not necessarily because they are smarter. They get in on deals before anyone else. We think that many asset owners fail to recognize how these structural advantages are developed, maintained and then used. The bigger issue is that they don't even consider the structural alpha they can generate themselves. Solution: they need to take innovation and creativity seriously. They need an R&D function that puts into play their structural advantages. One innovation is, itself, collaboration.

This chapter considered the practical and feasible ways to deploy assets in more efficient and effective ways, or rather, how to unleash structural alpha. Whether the path is alliances, syndicates or seeds (or some combination), the launch of these vehicles represents a groundbreaking first step towards a new model of institutional investment that serves the interests of the institutions and its stakeholders. We continue this discussion in Chap. 6, rehearsing the experience of an alliance of three sovereign wealth funds to tap early-stage innovations.

5

Unleashing Locational Advantage

If a reorganization of the functional and spatial structure of institutional invest-ment offers some new ways to align interests, it also poses profound organiza-tional and governance challenges. Indeed, the shifts in investment philosophy and execution that characterize innovative beneficiary institutions pose chal-lenges and complications for investment organizations, some of which result from the loss of economies of agglomeration. Large financial centres, such as New York, London and Honk Kong, gain many benefits from agglomera-tion, such as deep labour markets, a range of complementary services, and knowledge spillovers. As previous chapters have highlighted, attracting and retaining skilled and specialized workers, and accessing sufficient and attrac-tive deal flows, are easier to achieve in international financial centres than in other locations. As such, insourcing asset management poses challenges associated with a loss of the networks of agents in the major centres. Similarly, working creatively with asset managers—either through separate accounts or co-investment platforms—demands a level of face-to-face interaction that can be difficult to achieve from staff located back at the head office.

Face-to-face contact has been shown to be extremely important in envi-ronments where information is imperfect, rapidly changing and not easily codified. The most powerful mechanism to verify the intentions of some-one is direct face-to-face contact. Such interaction can help solve incentive problems, facilitate socialization and learning, and provide motivation and the development of trust.[1] Given this, it is not surprising that studies have

---

[1] Michael Storper and Anthony J. Venables, *Buzz: face-to-face contact and the urban economy*, 4 Journal of Economic Geography (2004).

© The Editor(s) (if applicable) and The Author(s) 2016
J. Singh Bachher et al., *The New Frontier Investors*,
DOI 10.1057/978-1-137-50857-7_5

shown that fund managers earn substantial abnormal returns when making investments close to home (up to 3 per cent higher). These returns are particularly strong among funds that are small, focus on few holdings, and operate out of remote areas.[2] This indicates that local investors with informational advantages are better at pricing assets and identifying valuable opportunities. This advantage may stem from the improved monitoring capabilities of local managers and investments, or access to private information of firms nearby. In sum, having local presence and face-to-face contacts can greatly enhance returns in regions and asset classes where informational asymmetries exist. This builds trust between the local players/authorities and the investor, as well as sending a signal of the investor's intentions.

As portfolios have grown more complicated over the past few decades, collecting the necessary information—especially qualitative—has grown more difficult. Nonetheless, a factor underpinning the success of certain investment strategies will be the collection of data, the processing of information, and the formulation of knowledge upon which investment decisions can be based. The conversion of information into knowledge is a crucial determinant of investment returns, as it affords investors the capacity to adapt investment strategies to the changing circumstances in local regions. One way that some investors are trying to address the challenges in gaining access to local knowledge and deal flows is by opening satellite offices in places where local knowledge is vital but information transfer is constrained. While this strategy comes with its own challenges, which we articulate below, expanding geographically can help beneficiary investors overcome the constraints of more active investing, either directly or through closer engagement with managers. At its core, such expansion can be seen as an investment operation and a risk mitigation function.[3]

Some frontier investors are thus establishing more satellite offices in international and regional financial centres, as well as in commercially important cities, which we refer to as non-financial centres. These foreign investors are seeking to become local investors with all the informational and investment advantages that come along with this status.[4] As noted above, having a local

---

[2] Joshua D. Coval and Tobias J. Moskowitz, *The geography of investment: informed trading and asset prices*, 109 JOURNAL OF POLITICAL ECONOMY (2001).

[3] We do not want to be too prescriptive here. Some beneficiary investors may find the logistical challenge of setting up a foreign office to be overly complex, or unnecessary for achieving their goals. There may be a stronger case for taking advantage of opportunities closer to home. Moreover, expanding geographically may be achieved via deeper peer relationships with like-minded institutions elsewhere, as we argued in the previous chapter.

[4] Christopher J. Malloy, *The geography of equity analysis*, 60 THE JOURNAL OF FINANCE (2005).

presence and face-to-face contacts can greatly enhance returns in regions and asset classes where informational asymmetries exist.

This chapter discusses the goals, challenges and lessons of geographic expansion in the formation of satellite offices. The arguments presented here are based on interviews with senior executives at 12 large pension and sovereign funds that have launched or have considered launching satellite offices. Readers should note that we sought a representative sample including those with several satellite offices as well as those that decided against setting up such offices. Among those that did have satellites, we also focused on those that set up offices in major IFCs as well those that had offices in cities not usually associated with large capital markets—or non-financial centres.[5]

The Goals of Geographic Expansion

There are various reasons why an institutional investor might want to set up a satellite office, such as monitoring managers more closely, obtaining proximity to deal flow, or collecting data in informationally inefficient markets. Based on our research, however, we identified two sets of thinking that seem to guide the decision to set up a satellite: those that provide a basis to set up an office in an IFC and those that favour an office in a non-financial centre. It is important to separate these two arguments, because the motivations and challenges for creating satellites in IFCs are different from those for non-financial centres. In the subsections below, we focus on the lessons learned from our case studies in these two domains. Table 5.1 provides some examples of satellite office formation.

International Financial Centres

There are a variety of goals and objectives that our case studies highlighted when describing their motivation for setting up an office in an IFC:

- *Attracting skilled workers*: As noted in the previous chapter, institutions based on the frontiers of finance have a limited labour pool. While this risk is reduced by their ability to attract certain types of employees, specialized expertise may still be hard to come by. Therefore, opening an office in a

---

[5] By IFC we refer to New York, London, Hong Kong and Singapore. Examples of non-financial centres are places such as Beijing, Chennai, São Paulo, and San Francisco, which are important regional financial centres, but they are not generally global hubs for deal flow and human resources.

Table 5.1 Satellite office formation

Institution name	Offices
Australian Super	Melbourne
Ontario Teachers' Pension Plan	Ontario, Beijing, Hong Kong, London
Korea Investment Corporation	Seoul, New York, London
Canada Pension Plan Investment Board	Toronto, Hong Kong, London
Kuwait Investment Authority	Kuwait, Beijing, London
Alberta Investment Management Corporation	Edmonton, Toronto, London
China Investment Corporation	Beijing, Hong Kong, Toronto
Norges Bank Investment Management	Oslo, New York, London, Shanghai, Singapore
Government of Singapore Investment Corporation	Singapore, Mumbai, London, Shanghai, Beijing, Seoul, Tokyo, San Francisco, New York
Temasek	Singapore, Mumbai, London, São Paulo, Mexico, Hanoi, Beijing, Ho Chi Minh, New York, Chennai, Hong Kong

major financial centre affords institutions access to a deeper and wider labour pool. Talented people in these markets can be expensive, but competitive salaries when combined with some of the additional benefits of working for a large asset owner (such as no fund raising and job security) can present a compelling option.

- *Deal flow*: Many funds are moving assets in-house with a view to making direct investments; these 'insourcers' believe they can operate at a lower cost and generate better net returns than external managers. At the same time, more funds are moving from public to private markets and investment in real estate and infrastructure, exploiting their long-term horizons to increase returns. For these investors, it can be useful to have an office in a major financial centre, as it offers a considerable amount of face-to-face interaction with peers, bankers and brokers who operate there.

- *Monitoring investment*: beneficiary institutions often use external managers to manage at least some of their assets, whether in public or private markets. Many of these managers and funds are based in major financial centres. Having such an office improves the monitoring of existing fund managers and helps when conducting due diligence to hire managers. Co-location also facilitates co-investment opportunities when they arise. The added value of this monitoring becomes even more critical when one considers the principle-agent problems that exist from hiring external managers. Face-to-face contact has the potential to increase the efficiency of communication; solve incentive problems; facilitate socialization and learning; and it provides psychological motivation. Deal-making, evaluation and relationship adjustment depend on face-to-face contact.

- *Cooperation*: research shows that proximity affects network formation, and being in the same place can improve collaboration between institutions.[6] Launching a satellite office in an IFC can help expand an institution's global network and reinforce communication with like-minded, long-term-oriented investment institutions that have done the same. This might even give rise to investment vehicles, such as alliances and syndicates that could be domiciled in those cities.

- *Retaining staff*: institutions on the frontiers of finance complained about the difficulty of holding on to investment professionals beyond 3–5 years. Having an office in or close to a financial centre can help to retain such people back at the head office for longer periods of time, because there is perceived to be an option to move to the satellite office at some point,

---

[6] H. Bathelt and J. Glückler, THE RELATIONAL ECONOMY: GEOGRAPHIES OF KNOWING AND LEARNING (Oxford University Press, 2011).

either permanently or for periods of time. Having a satellite office can decrease the cost as well as the wear and tear that continuous travelling has on employees, which in turn has the potential to increase the quality of life for employees. Indeed, certain jurisdictions (e.g. the European Union) require physical presence at investment fund board meetings, which may occur frequently. Sending a representative from a nearby satellite office (e.g. from London to Luxembourg) economizes on personal and work time much more than having to send a representative from the head office, which may be in another continent.

- *Knowledge transfer*: being in the region where there is a cluster of financial workers should result in knowledge development and transfer. Many institutional investors are already leveraging their relationship with existing external managers to help train their employees. Having an office in London or New York should substantially increase that potential knowledge transfer. The circulation of workers between institutions enhances the ability of these institutions to recombine knowledge and imitate best practices. Employees can absorb knowledge from contact with more skilled individuals in their own industry. The number of probable contacts an individual makes is a function of the size of the financial centre. Taking this one step further, those employees could then transfer that knowledge back to the head office, which in turn will be transferred to the co-workers there.

Non-financial Centres

In our case studies, interviewees highlighted a variety of goals and objectives when describing their motivation for setting up an office in a non-financial centre:

- *Local knowledge*: having offices in non-financial centres enables institutions to gauge more accurately what is happening in a region, rather than relying only on official statistics and data. This is particularly useful in emerging and frontier economies, as well as dynamic market environments, where it is difficult to predict where future investment opportunities will come from. Moreover, it potentially reduces the investor's reliance on third parties for data and information.
- *Deal flow*: some non-financial centres may be in places with underdeveloped public markets. Having an office in an non-financial centre aids access to unlisted investments, such as real estate but also private equity, without using intermediaries.

- *Networks of influence*: investing in foreign countries—especially through direct private investments—exposes institutions to headline risk. This risk can be mitigated by signalling to the region a certain level of organizational commitment. Opening a satellite office and hiring locals sends such a signal and makes institutions visible in the local market. Being physically present in a region also increases an institution's ability to build relationships with local players that can assist in the investment process. This is specifically important in non-financial centres where local networks play a key role in sourcing and executing investment opportunities.
- *Politics*: in many emerging markets, government investment and expenditure remains the largest source of investment in the country and ministers are seeking external investors as co-investors. The signalling effect of opening a local office in the country might pave the way to better relationships with the local government.
- *Next-best alternative*: some of our respondents indicated that they decided to open a satellite office in an non-financial centre because they needed to recruit additional talent or have a more central location with proximity to managers and opportunities, but could not afford to move to an IFC. The idea of going to a non-financial centre was to have a more central location that could offer some of the benefits of having an office in an IFC, but without the drawbacks of being in an IFC (such as higher costs and the higher competition for talent). This secondary location could also help retain some employees by decreasing the time they spend travelling and basing them in a larger city.

The Challenges of Geographic Expansion

Clearly, there are sound reasons for a beneficiary institution to consider setting up a satellite office in IFCs and non-financial centres. At the same time, however, our case studies flagged up constraints and challenges that all funds should take into consideration. Once again, we consider the cases of IFCs and non-financial centres in turn.

International Finance Centres

Our interviewees indicated several challenges in trying to launch satellite offices in IFCs.

- *Loss of staff*: people would appear to be both a benefit and a risk of setting up an office in an IFC. As it turns out, the private sector often has the capacity to pay higher wages than the public pension funds or sovereign wealth funds that are setting up satellite offices. As such, the non-local offices can become a revolving door for staff; a sort of holding tank for individuals before they move back to private sector opportunities. Indeed, portfolio managers with a few years of experience at a large pension or sovereign fund will be a prime target for investment banks and other private institutions.

- *Costs*: opening an office in a financial centre will also be costly. Not only will a fund need to pay higher salaries, but it will have to bear the extra costs of sending someone from the head office to live there (and living costs may be higher than in the home country). In addition, the organization must consider the legal as well as the political costs of opening a satellite office.
- *Governance and culture*: governance of satellite offices is another challenge, because integrating satellite offices into the organizational hierarchy often requires more reporting lines and delegated authorities. There is also a risk that the culture of the main office will not transfer to the new office. These issues might give rise to tensions and clashes between the head office and the satellite offices. This can also lead to investment risk, be that in the inability of the head office to effectively monitor the dealings of the satellite office, the inefficient exchange of information between the offices, or the pressure that the satellite office might feel to execute deals (i.e., if you give them a bucket, they will go ahead and fill it up).

Non-financial Centres

Again, there are challenges and risks with setting up a satellite in an non-financial centre.

- *Culture and governance*: as with IFCs, this is a challenge. But this risk is amplified when opening offices in non-financial centres, especially in areas where the local culture and norms are different from the home institution. A simple rule such as 'not accepting a potential business partner's invitation to dinner' can be a problem if applied, for example, in Asia. The key here is to try to strike a balance between trying to export as much of the head office culture and governance protocols to the satellite office without hindering its effectiveness to operate in the local market. Indeed, some of the funds we spoke to cited this as one of the main reasons for not opening an office in a non-financial centre.
- *Scalability*: many of the institutions we spoke to mentioned this as one of the main factors in deciding where to open an office. Many non-financial

centres in emerging markets, while growing, have a long way to go before offering the depth of market found in more advanced economies. This raises important issues. For one, the setup and operating costs of the satellite office need to be weighed against the size of the investment opportunities. If the potential scale of asset deployment is small, the cost of a satellite office may outweigh, or at least diminish, the returns it generates. Likewise, if investment opportunities are limited, will satellite offices feel pressure to invest in sub-par investments, as a means of justifying their existence? Yet, even if scalability is limited initially, the long-term growth trajectory could be such that scale emerges over time. Setting up a satellite office may provide first-mover advantages to those funds that establish an early presence in the market. Some organizations may not, however, have sufficient resolve to see the satellite office through its initial establishment and potentially several years of lacklustre performance, particularly if early proponents of establishing the satellite office leave the organization.

Geographic Expansion: Key Lessons

Based on the case studies and a detailed review of the literature, we think there is a simple set of lessons and questions that can inform and guide the process of considering a non-local office.

Governance and Culture

Many of our respondents cited that the main challenge in opening a satellite office as being how to govern the office, be it in controlling the investment process or in ensuring that the mentality, goals and policies were in line with the main office. This issue was especially prevalent when opening an office in countries where the business and cultural norms are different from the home country. Here are some of the ways in which organizations have tackled this problem:

- Having employees work at the headquarters for several years (usually around 3 years) before being posted to a different office.
- Sending a senior member from headquarters to the new office for extended periods of time. This will ensure that the office is set up in a way that is aligned with the intuitions, goals and policies of the sponsoring fund.
- Keeping investment decisions centralized, so that the final say on any investment remains with the head office. (However, this may hamstring the ability of the local team to build meaningful, trustworthy relationships

with local teams, as the head office may veto deals that the local investors have worked hard pulling together.)

- Maintaining some flexibility that allows the satellite office to be culturally different. After all, the purpose of the satellite office is at times to embed the team in a foreign culture, which may mean deviating from some of the head office processes.

Alignment with Fund Strategy

Opening a satellite office requires commitment from the management and the board. As a result, it is critical to demonstrate that opening such an office is fundamental to achieving the long-term objectives of the fund. Managers and the board should, therefore, have a clear answer to each of the following questions:

- Is the organization planning to move some of the investment management function in-house? If so, there may be a benefit in setting up a satellite to gain proximity to deal flow, information and talent (this is especially true in private, illiquid markets).
- Is the organization planning to work with external managers in creative ways that demand more monitoring? If so, it may be valuable to facilitate routine face-to-face contact.
- Is the organization planning to invest in regions where information flows are inefficient and thus local knowledge is key? If so, it may be valuable to establish a local presence.

Setting Goals

Organizations should be clear about the motivation and goals of opening a satellite office. Some questions to consider are:

- Is the organization trying to gain access to a deeper talent pool? If so, does the organization have a pay structure that can attract the best people in an IFC? If not, perhaps a non-financial centre is more appropriate.
- Is the organization trying to increase retention of employees? If so, it may be valuable to offer options for living away from the head office.
- Is the organization trying to capitalize on the local workforce and local knowledge in informational inefficient regions? It may be important to set up in a non-financial centre.

- Is the organization trying to increase its efficiency by positioning itself closer to assets or to intermediaries with purview of those assets? It may be important to set up in an IFC.

In answering these questions, investors should be able to triangulate back to the non-financial centre, IFC, or 'do not expand' options.

Staffing

An issue that many of our respondents faced when opening a satellite office is how to staff it. Should they have employees from the head office posted there, or should they hire local employees? Each of these options has pros and cons. For example, staffing the office with people from the head office will make it easier to transfer the culture and governance to the satellite office; it will also help align the investment goals with the head office. On the other hand, local employees will increase the effectiveness of the office in obtaining information as well as capitalizing on local knowledge. Our respondents have found that staffing the office depends on the answers to some of the following questions:

- What are the goals of opening the office? See above.
- Where will the new office be located? In an IFC it may be valuable to send staff from the head office, while in an non-financial centre it may be valuable to have a mix of local and the head office staff.
- What are the resources and talent available in the head office and can they be deployed abroad effectively? Does the fund have people with the necessary language skills?
- What are the policies for compensation? Again, this will influence the kind of people that can be recruited in establishing an office in IFCs.

Politics

Another issue cited by respondents was the political challenges in opening offices abroad, especially in emerging markets, from national or local governments as well as local business investors. Some ways in which these issues were addressed were:

- Collaborating with the home country's local embassy.
- Hiring locals in managerial positions.
- Co-investing with local governments, investors and institutions.

Scalability

Opening a satellite office is costly and requires substantial time, effort and money. A key factor in determining where to open an office for many of our respondents was the potential for investment opportunities over time. As such, answering the following questions may be useful:

- What are the potential asset classes and industries that could be accessed through the new office? If there is potential for real estate, timber and infrastructure along with public and private markets, then this can be attractive.
- What are the markets that can be credibly managed out of the new office? There are locations that offer access to numerous countries.

Conclusions

We have outlined in this chapter reasons why funds have considered opening a satellite office, including: access to talent, knowledge development and transfers, manager/investment monitoring, access to investment opportunities and deal flow, information gathering and risk management. However, this road is fraught with difficulties and complexities including: governance, culture, management of employees, costs, resources and political risks. For organizations undergoing internal transformations, setting up an overseas office may be a step too far because it is incredibly important to have the main office functioning effectively before opening more offices.

Indeed, to open offices successfully, managers should verify that the institution possesses strong governance and an organizational culture that can be transferred. Furthermore, in deciding whether or not to open an office as well as deciding where to open one, managers should reflect on the long-term strategy of the fund and think of what elements are required to achieve that strategy and relate that to the goals of opening an office. This perhaps seems overly simplistic in terms of a conclusion, but we were surprised more than once by the dearth of 'grand planning' that took place before going ahead with a satellite office, oftentimes in an IFC.

Despite these complexities, opening a satellite office may be beneficial in the long term, as even a small increase in returns stemming from local knowledge can far outweigh the costs and resources needed. Additionally, these satellite offices can provide institutions with access to talent pools not available at headquarters. A satellite office can also position institutions closer to their investments and external managers, improving supervision and the efficiency of risk management. However, we also want to stress that setting up an office overseas may not be the right decision or desirable for all beneficiary institutions. Collaboration with peers may be, in that case, the way to expand geographically. Having outlined collaboration in Chap. 4, we expand on that discussion in the next chapter.

6

The Valley of Opportunity: Bringing Innovation to Venture Capital

Venture capital investing has been an unsatisfactory experience for many long-term institutional investors (LTIs). First, the asset class has not performed in line with expectations for more than a decade. For example, these investors have given more money to venture capitalists since 1997, in aggregate, than they have had in return over that period.[1] Second, even among the top decile, managers that have demonstrated the (rare) ability to outperform VC benchmarks consistently, there have been few opportunities for newer or slower-moving investors to access their funds. As such, VC as an asset class has really only worked for those investors that were first in, such as endowments and family offices, because they have managed to hold on to their allocations at the top VCs. In large part, the challenges associated with this asset class stem from the fact that VC investing does not scale easily.

Venture capital is an investment industry with high labour intensity. This stems from the fact that venture investing is largely a services business founded on high-touch interaction with entrepreneurs through trusted (and hard-earned) networks. And the best venture capital firms tend to view their job as business development rather than passive investment organizations. And herein lies the irony of today's venture capital industry: the best VCs are very capable at helping entrepreneurs scale their businesses, but they have not been able to bring scale to their own industry without eroding

---

[1] D. Mulcahy, et al., WE HAVE MET THE ENEMY AND HE IS US: LESSONS FROM TWENTY YEARS OF THE KAUFFMAN FOUNDATION'S INVESTMENT IN VENTURE CAPITAL FUNDS AND THE TRIUMPH OF HOPE OVER EXPERIENCE (Ewing Marion Kauffman Foundation. 2012).

© The Editor(s) (if applicable) and The Author(s) 2016
J. Singh Bachher et al., *The New Frontier Investors*,
DOI 10.1057/978-1-137-50857-7_6

performance.[2] In fact, many VCs have given up trying to expand their businesses, purposely keeping the size of their funds small to focus on their core area of expertise: helping entrepreneurs launch and build companies.

This keep-it-small mentality, however, means that venture capital has not had the capacity to accommodate the demands of LTIs. After all, an allocation of $10–$20 million to a top VC's fund won't move the needle on returns for a large pension or sovereign fund even if the underlying investments are highly successful. Moreover, spreading a large VC allocation across a large number of asset managers will result in an institutional investor paying high fees for beta exposure to the asset class. This is not attractive. As a result, LTIs are now asking themselves, 'What's the point?' In fact, public pension funds and sovereign funds have been reducing their venture capital commitments to external managers and, instead, have been focusing on alternative asset classes that can offer economies of scale.

While we understand the logic above, we nonetheless believe there is an opportunity for LTIs to re-engage with venture investing in a meaningful way. Consider that over the period that VC returns have struggled, innovation and technological development has not stopped. In fact, the rate of innovation, if anything, has continued to accelerate, changing the lives of people in meaningful ways (via the iPhone, iPad, Facebook, Android, Kindle, electric car, etc.). Ultimately, huge value is still being created through technological innovation, which suggests to us that VC investing still has value to offer LTIs. However, making VC work demands an innovative approach. As such, large investors that do find ways to access this asset class offer useful case studies of innovation at the core of institutional investment and asset management.

For LTIs to participate in VC in an aligned and scalable way, they need to participate only in those sectors where they can add value, because it's in these domains where they can get better alignment of interests with managers and entrepreneurs. In our experience, there are two domains where institutional investors can add value. First, there is a compelling case for LTIs to participate in the venture capital of financial services (e.g., fintech) and asset management (e.g., invest-tech). Pensions and sovereigns not only have considerable expertise in these two areas, but they also have the ability to deliver cornerstone clients to their portfolio of firms. Second, a long-term, capital-endowed player can serve as a bridge for growth-stage companies. Said differently, making venture capital work for LTIs, such as pensions and sovereign funds, means finding certain verticals in which the portfolio companies cannot rely on venture managers alone to reach commercial scale. Clearly, this

---

[2] Size of fund has been shown to influence performance over the long term, S. N. Kaplan and A. Schoar, *Private Equity Performance: Returns, Persistence, and Capital Flows*, 60 The Journal of Finance (2005).

has been the case in capital-intensive industries. As such, we argue that LTIs may be uniquely positioned to participate in areas where they can serve as this bridge from VCs to public markets. We also believe that the principles of this approach are applicable in other asset classes and could serve to help asset owners develop their own 'structural alpha'.

In the last decade, VCs added 'green' to their staples of information technology and biotech investments. What they found in doing green investments, however, was that the time horizon to profitability was far longer than they had anticipated. VCs often reached a point where their companies' future was dependent on finding another set of investors that could 'take the baton' forward and develop the 'green infrastructure' that was often required. This was a big problem for the VCs, and it left many of them feeling much like the entrepreneurs that approach them: they were forced to look for somebody else to fund their big idea through to commercial scale. In this sense, the green-tech strategy by VCs has offered LTIs a chance to re-engage with this asset class. Moreover, it offers a way to bring scale to venture capital, particularly in capital-intensive industries such as energy, materials, food and water, as the time horizon and size of LTIs afford the possibility of funding capital-intensive companies all the way to commercial scale.[3]

Hence, venture capital is an asset class that still offers opportunity for intrepid institutional investors. It simply needs these institutions to consider their own competitive advantages before engaging in the asset class. Indeed, the juxtaposition of large VC losses coming from green investments with the potential for enormous future gains presents an interesting opportunity. Indeed, we think LTIs can serve as important bridges for venture-backed, capital-intensive companies looking to get to commercial scale, and they can, in turn, participate in the success of these companies over the long term. Rather than seeing a 'valley of death' for capital-intensive companies, we see a 'valley of opportunity'.

The Valley of Death

At the earliest stages of launching a company, investors are asked to provide capital to a venture that has no products and sometimes no markets for future products; there is just an entrepreneur's vision for what the company can develop into and how that company can, in turn, generate returns. Assuming the entrepreneur secures funding to launch a company, it can take years before products come to market and cash flows turn from negative to positive.

---

[3] In 2008, the traditional partners of VCs, such as endowments, demonstrated an inability to participate in co-investments because of liquidity constraints. This has opened up the opportunity to other, longer-term investors such as pensions and sovereign funds.

This period before reaching commercial scale is one in which companies are reliant on external financing to fund operations. This vulnerable period is sometimes referred to as the valley of death because it is in this phase that most companies fail.[4]

While the valley of death technically affects all companies, those operating in industries with high capital inputs are perceived to be particularly vulnerable.[5] In economic jargon, the standard J-curve applicable to venture investments in sectors such as energy, food and water, tends to run deeper and longer than is the case for generic venture investments in industries such as software.[6] It's perhaps not surprising then that green companies that rely on private financing find it difficult to reach commercial scale, as the average green energy venture has required $500 million from investors before commercialization.[7] Given that companies only begin to exit the valley of death when commercialization starts to take hold, and entrepreneurs demonstrate a clear path to profitability (and steady cash flows), companies in capital-intensive industries are more prone to failure in the valley of death than those in less capital-intensive industries.[8]

It's little wonder that the green revolution that overwhelmed the venture capital community in the last decade has thus far generated so few success stories. In our view, the traditional model of venture capital does not lend itself as easily to capital-intensive industries, such as energy innovation, as it does to capital-light industries, such as software. A traditional venture capital firm raises money from individuals and institutions to invest in early-stage ventures that are high-risk and have high-expected returns.[9] The general partner (GP) raises $300–$600 million from limited partners (LPs) for an investment fund.[10] With this capital, a VC will typically invest in 15–30 companies, and the initial investments range between $5 million and $20 million.[11] This

[4] Paul A. Gompers and Josh Lerner, *What drives venture capital fundraising?*, NBER WORKING PAPERS (1999).

[5] Ramana Nanda et al., *Innovation and entrepreneurship in renewable energy, in* THE CHANGING FRONTIER: RETHINKING SCIENCE AND INNOVATION POLICY (2014).

[6] P.Y. Mathonet and T. Meyer, J-CURVE EXPOSURE: MANAGING A PORTFOLIO OF VENTURE CAPITAL AND PRIVATE EQUITY FUNDS (John Wiley & Sons, 2008).

[7] Andrew B. Hargadon and Martin Kenney, *Misguided policy? Following venture capital into clean technology*, 54 CALIFORNIA MANAGEMENT REVIEW (2012).

[8] L. Murphy and P. Edwards, BRIDGING THE VALLEY OF DEATH: TRANSITIONING FROM PUBLIC TO PRIVATE SECTOR FINANCING (National Renewable Energy Laboratory, 2003).

[9] William A. Sahlman, *The structure and governance of venture-capital organizations*, 27 JOURNAL OF FINANCIAL ECONOMICS (1990).

[10] See Kenney R. Florida and M. Kenney, *Venture capital, high technology and regional development*, 22 REGIONAL STUDIES (1988).

[11] Bob Zider, *How venture capital works*, 76 HARVARD BUSINESS REVIEW (1998).

then allows for as much as $20 million to $30 million in follow-up funding for the most promising three to five ventures.

By necessity, then, a large majority of successful venture capital exits have been capital-light.[12] In fact, the most successful venture investments tend to be those where less than $30 million was invested before commercial scale was achieved and cash flows turned positive. In fact, 79 of the 98 venture-capital backed 'exits' in the second quarter of 2013 were in the capital-light information technology sector.[13] Google is the classic example of a capital-light venture, because it raised only about $25 million before its market listing.[14] If we compare Google's path to success with that of Tesla, the darling of the green movement, it is easy to see the diametrically opposed cash flow profiles of these two companies. In year seven of operations, Tesla lost $396 million, having lost almost $1 billion in total. As for Google, it was profitable in its third year and generated $1.4 billion in net income in year seven.

As such, while the VC community is renowned for taking fledgling innovations and developing businesses around them, this has not held true for the capital-intensive green movement. This can be partially attributed to a mediocre market for initial public offerings (IPOs), which has a strong influence on VC returns. But we see this as also being the result of a fundamental incongruence between the characteristics of a capital-intensive green investment and the monetary resources of venture capital funds. In short, the time horizon and capital intensity of green venture investments has rendered venture capitals less effective at 'picking winners' as they have been in the past with other industries.[15] To a large extent, this stems from the fact that VCs are attempting to 'disrupt' the built infrastructure of the economy without recognizing that enormous pools of capital are required to do so. As such, they had to rely on other parties and investors to help them bring their capital-intensive portfolio companies to commercial scale. Once again, this left VCs, like their portfolio companies, vulnerable to the valley of death.

Given the disappointing returns VCs have reaped from their green investments over the past decade (especially compared with the remarkable returns in previous decades), many VCs have sought to cultivate additional pools of

[12] Robert Wiltbank and Warren Boeker, *Angel investor performance project: data overview* at http://ssrn.com/abstract=1024714

[13] See, http://thomsonreuters.com/content/dam/openweb/documents/pdf/corporate/press-releases/q2-13-exits-release.pdf

[14] David A. Vise and Mark Malseed, THE GOOGLE STORY-INSIDE THE HOTTEST BUSINESS, MEDIA AND TECHNOLOGY SUCCESS OF OUR TIMES (Pan Macmillan, 2006).

[15] Alfred Marcus et al., *The Promise and Pitfalls of Venture Capital as an Asset Class for Clean Energy Investment Research Questions for Organization and Natural Environment Scholars*, 26 ORGANIZATION & ENVIRONMENT (2013).

external capital to help them bring their companies to scale. In general, they have turned to three sources of capital:

- *Government*: national governments have been a key backer of technological innovation, especially at the riskiest levels of intellectual property development. And, as such, many VCs cultivate relationships with governments to secure funding for their companies, even launching lobbying efforts and participating in government as advisors. However, in the current political climate (especially in the US), this is a controversial path; there is little appetite among taxpayers to see their government 'picking winners' (and more so losers) by giving loan guarantees to private companies.[16]
- *Syndicates of VCs*: many VCs have looked to one another to help pool capital for portfolio companies. However, even when syndicating across venture capital funds, as suggested by Lerner (1994) and Lockett and Wright (2001), there remains a funding gap for capital-intensive companies to scale up. Indeed, the more successful cleantech and green energy companies have required a billion dollars or more, which is beyond the reach of even syndicates of VCs.
- *Syndicates of other investors*: syndicates of other types of investors can work, such as bringing banks, growth-stage PE investors and project financiers together in a transaction. However, the coordination challenges of bringing these disparate investors together are immense, and most of these investor types bring with them different objective functions and incentives that can derail the long-term plans of a company. Moreover, in an increasingly short-term market, most investors view capital-intensive investments, such as green ventures, as unattractive. Certain investors are further constrained by mandate to invest in specific products or strategies that are not readily applied to the green sector, which often combines aspects of venture capital, private equity and infrastructure into a single transaction.

So, it's quite difficult to identify groups of financial investors that could credibly work alongside VCs to finance these capital-intense ventures through to commercial scale. In the section that follows, we provide a case for working with LTIs.

---

[16] The US administration received particular criticism for its $535 million loan guarantee given to now bankrupt solar company, Solyndra, with a government committee accusing the Department of Energy of negligence and mismanagement (2012). This has led to less government support for capital-intensive companies; see Daniel R. Cahoy, *Inverse enclosure: abdicating the green technology landscape*, 49 AMERICAN BUSINESS LAW JOURNAL (2012).

The Valley of Opportunity

Notwithstanding past failures, it is reasonable to suggest that a select number of capital-intensive ventures will, in the years ahead, revolutionize antiquated industries by becoming commercially viable and indeed scalable companies. Due to the combined effects of climate change and resource scarcity, the green economy is almost certainly not a passing fad. Quite the contrary, we believe that a subset of the green energy and technology companies of this generation will go on to be the most profitable companies for generations to come. And it is this juxtaposition of large past losses next to the potential for future gains that we believe creates an opening for LTIs; we call this the 'valley of opportunity'.

The problems that capital-intensive industries create for the VC industry actually serve the interests of LTIs. In fact, there are tangible examples of the institutional investment community, and in particular pension and sovereign funds, participating as key financiers of innovative companies and projects (both on the equity and debt side) that sit between venture capital, private equity and infrastructure (see the Innovation Alliance case study below). And yet, for LTIs to take advantage of this situation, they need to re-conceptualize the way they access VC opportunities. Too many pensions or sovereign funds want VC to be easy, but making VC work for LTIs requires far more than writing a cheque and then crossing fingers. It requires meaningful engagement with the asset class and the companies therein.

We have identified three innovative ways in which LTIs are attempting to participate in VC in a more aligned and scalable manner: [17]

- *Direct*: a few institutional investors are bringing VC investing in house, building on their experience of direct private equity and direct infrastructure to do direct venture investing in creative ways. The fund that stands out in this regard is the Ontario Municipal Employees Retirement System (OMERS), which had, at the time of our research in 2013, a team of 14 people doing direct VC deals in the US and Canada. They made a name for themselves as one of the 'go to VCs' for Canadian entrepreneurs. And they began to manage capital for third parties. This is an attractive model, if you can recruit the necessary people to run such a programme, because it can solve the time horizon problem; OMERS can continue to invest in the portfolio companies as they develop. And that also solves the scale prob-

---

[17] A health warning applies to these approaches. Investing directly in venture-stage companies within a public fund requires a high level of commitment and understanding on the part of the board. Some investments will, inevitably, fail. That's the nature of the asset class. Boards need to be prepared for this. The hope is that you have more winners than losers so the net effect on the portfolio is positive.

lem, because the winners coming out of the VC portfolio will require ever-larger amounts of capital. Conceivably, the biggest winners coming out of the venture portfolio could be seamlessly passed into the public equity portfolios and even handed off to fixed income teams.

- *Seeding*: some funds have taken to seeding new managers to achieve the alignment of interests and scale they want from this asset class. The example that jumps to mind is the Wellcome Trust, which recently seeded a $325 million venture capital business that will back biotechnology startups. The outfit is called Syncona Partners, and it's being structured as an 'evergreen investment company.' This approach offers many of the benefits of an in-house VC practice, while still offering the flexibility required to attract talented workers. In addition, this vehicle is particularly interesting because it exploits the unique skill set of the Wellcome Trust, which is a charity focused on healthcare. As such, building a venture practice around healthcare is probably smart from the perspective of asymmetric information and deal flow.
- *Creative collaboration*: some VCs and LTIs have sought to form deep relationships with one another. The VCs look to pension funds and sovereign wealth funds (SWFs) to help bring their most promising companies across the finish line, while the funds look to the VCs to provide a more aligned access point for the asset class than they have in the past. In addition, the pensions and sovereigns will often work with each other in creative ways, recognizing that the success of these collaborative arrangements will only work if they can credibly assess the companies presented by the VCs.

In all cases, whether it's an in-house portfolio, seeding a manager, or working with peers and managers in creative ways to back growth-stage companies, LTIs that can find the people to run a direct or hybrid programme have a remarkable opportunity in VC today. Among these three paths, we have spent the most time examining and understanding 'creative collaboration'. The case study below demonstrates how VC can work for LTIs.

The Innovation Alliance

In late 2012, three sovereign wealth funds signed a memorandum of understanding to invest jointly in growth capital opportunities globally. This group was called the Innovation Alliance and included the New Zealand Super Fund, the Alberta Investment Management Corporation (AIMCo) and the Abu Dhabi Investment Authority (ADIA). The alliance was set up to make the most of the members' long-term investment horizons, global networks and large pools of capital to help build disruptive companies in capital-starved industries. As far as we know, this was the first co-investment vehicle created to offer sovereign funds the chance to cherry pick the best opportunities in top VC portfolios. By committing to the alliance, the sovereigns were seeking to increase its investment options and alignment, while reducing its costs. The alliance thus represents a valuable option (rather than an obligation) for the three sovereign funds. The rest of this section offers details of this unique case.

In launching the alliance, the members set out the investment beliefs that were driving them to launch a co-investment platform of this nature:

- LTIs could use the valley of death to their advantage, extracting investor-friendly terms from companies that could one day disrupt energy markets.
- They had a unique ability to make long-term commitments to illiquid investments, and making these commitments could result in higher returns.
- Pooling resources to vet opportunities was valuable, as venture capital tends to be a highly technical and non-standard asset class.
- Making direct VC investments was risky and expensive, which made an alliance with like-minded and deep-pocketed peers an attractive option as a way to diversify.
- Forging strategic relationships with best-in-class VC managers could lead to compelling investment opportunities with sustainable long-term returns.

When it came to strategy, the alliance sought direct investments in high-quality, late-stage, private, venture-backed companies that were emerging as 'the next big thing' in energy, food, and water industries. It would make size-able commitments ($50–$500 million per company of initial and follow-on capital) in a concentrated portfolio of five to ten companies. It was decided that the alliance would pay no fees.

As to implementation, one of the alliance members had a strong relation-ship with two top-decile, name-brand VCs. These were approached to see if a formal collaboration with the alliance was of interest. The offer was to provide the alliance unique and privileged access on a 'no fee or cost' basis. The alli-ance solidified these relationships through letters of intent to build companies in industries with high capital requirements, disproportionate advantages and long-term, market-validated growth. This relationship came with no explicit or even implicit fees or costs because the VCs and LTIs viewed this as a divi-sion of labour; the VCs assessed the technology risks and the alliance came in and helped the companies achieve commercial scale.

Administration was based around twice-yearly meetings in Silicon Valley between alliance members and the VCs. Monthly calls between the staff of the alliance and the VCs keep everyone abreast of developments in portfolio companies. Members share costs and expenses for due diligence as well as administration. The alliance was purposely kept to three funds at the outset to ensure effective and efficient execution. A very small number of new partners may be added in the years ahead, based on unanimous agreement among the founders. Investment decisions are all made individually for each case, but the members share the job of doing the analysis and due diligence.

The three peers made a notional commitment of $1 billion to the alliance. The idea here was to get organizational buy-in from each peer for what would be required to execute the strategy; a commitment (even if only notional) was a mechanism to trigger internal resourcing and planning.

To date, the alliance has deployed about $1 billion directly into green companies and projects.

Success Factors

What makes this model work, according to the alliance, was not being naive about the parties' motives (even if, in the end, the motives end up being pure). This 'partnership' only works if the alliance has the in-house skills to properly vet all the opportunities that the VCs bring. Without such skills, the partners would run into principal-agent problems and could end up helping VCs salvage their underperforming companies, which is clearly not what they want to do. With these factors in mind, the three SWFs teamed up, pooling their venture resources into a single team. They run all in-bound opportunities through this team and focus on executing a rigorous and meticulous evaluation of the opportunity. In addition, by focusing on industries that touch on infrastructure, the three SWFs can exploit their expertise in direct infrastructure investments. This has also been critical in vetting some of the opportunities presented to the alliance. So far, this collaboration has been rewarding, but all three members admit it's early days and the proof of this concept will be in the returns generated.

Lessons Learned

This section distills the lessons from the case studies and own experience studying and working with LTIs looking to leverage the valley of opportunity. We thus set out the principles and policies that we believe LTIs should focus on when considering (or managing the process of) investing in capital-intensive ventures. Readers will notice that the principles below highlight the cultural and theoretical challenges facing LTIs, while the policies focus on resolving operational and implementation challenges.

Principles

Making green investments means asking LTIs to step far outside their comfort zones, as the nature of the risks embedded in capital-intensive companies places them beyond the reach of traditional investors. As such, cultural and organizational adjustments may be required for institutional investors to succeed in financing green innovations. The following principles were deemed to be fundamental for allowing LTIs to invest in green VC opportunities:

1. *Responsibility*: the most challenging cultural change facing LTIs is, ironically, the need to take more responsibility for, and ownership over, the actual investments in their portfolio. Typically, institutional investors work through a long chain of intermediaries before their capital is actually deployed. But while this chain may make an allocator's job relatively easy, it also serves to neuter the competitive advantages of LTIs in this domain. For example, investing via external asset managers serves to shrink the time-horizon of the investment decision-making and distort the incentives and objectives of the ultimate asset owners. In short, LTIs need to be willing and able to make direct investments in green companies, which means they have to build in-house teams and capability. In this regard, governance is critical.

2. *Theory*: For investors relying on traditional portfolio and investment theories, it can be hard to justify growth-stage investing in green companies. As such, LTIs need to move beyond the commonly applied tenets of modern portfolio theory, as the traditional models and tools of portfolio management will always struggle to capture and articulate the value of these long-horizon, parametric innovations. In large part, this stems from the fact that a truly game-changing technology will create a new industry, not just a new firm. The entrepreneur(s) have to build a set of vendors and suppliers that will help the company scale up. Thus, the rigid metrics of modern portfolio theory are uneasily applied to these ventures, as modern portfolio theory does not take into account future increased earnings potential stemming from the opportunities to capture value along the path of building an entire industry, because of its reliance on rigid, quantifiable metrics. Therefore, instead of traditional theories, we believe that LTIs should use a hybrid

model that combines venture capital style assessments with more traditional PE and infrastructure metrics.[18]

3. *Risk*: When it comes to green ventures, LTIs often have to adopt a different mindset related to risk. In all likelihood, cash flows do not yet exist on a level that rationalizes the existing valuation, especially when set against comparable companies in other industries. What this requires then is an ability to look beyond the risks and focus on what's possible; they must view risk in a similar way to venture capitalists. This qualitative and subjective framing leaves many LTIs rather uncomfortable, but many successful green investments have required this sort of thinking on the part of the capital providers. (It has even been required for companies such as Amazon, which required enormous financial backing before finally turning a profit because of the infrastructure that had to be built by the company before profitability.) Note that qualitative and subjective need not imply a lack of rigour. Rather, the need is for bottom-up analysis and remarkable, in-depth, due diligence. In a certain manner of thinking, this is an approach that requires even more discipline and rigour than some of the traditional top-down models of investment decision-making.[19]

4. *Engagement*: It's important that LTIs recognize the importance and value of their engagement in the portfolio companies. Many companies view the manner in which institutional investors add value to be more critical than the cost of their capital.[20] And while LTIs often believe that they have little of value, we see a variety of ways they can assist in commercialization. Since LTIs have a large network of peers, they can provide important introductions to entities that can provide big sums of money, reducing the need to be in 'fundraising mode' for too long. They can also provide compelling introductions to potential customers or vendors. And, critically, LTIs can provide sufficient support and capital to help with transformations similar to those articulated in a seminal book, the *Innovator's Dilemma*.[21] Often, core business models need to be changed for businesses to remain competitive. We think that VCs and LTIs can both add value at different stages of a venture's lifespan.

---

[18] See, Joel A. C. Baum and Brian S. Silverman, *Picking winners or building them? Alliance, intellectual, and human capital as selection criteria in venture financing and performance of biotechnology startups*, 19 JOURNAL OF BUSINESS VENTURING (2004).

[19] LTIs should also develop a risk budget such that these high-risk investments don't put a huge strain on the portfolio. Since disruptive companies have idiosyncratic risk, risk can be managed through diversification.

[20] William D. Bygrave and Jeffry A. Timmons, VENTURE CAPITAL AT THE CROSSROADS (Harvard Business Press, 1992).

[21] Clayton Christensen, THE INNOVATOR'S DILEMMA: WHEN NEW TECHNOLOGIES CAUSE GREAT FIRMS TO FAIL (Harvard Business Review Press, 2013).

Policies

The following operational and strategic factors are deemed to be important for all LTIs looking at this type of investing:

1. *Direct investing*: for LTIs to be engaged in their investments, as well as have the capability to assess which green ventures have the most promise, they need to have organizational and human resources that match even the most sophisticated 'growth stage' investors. This implies the presence of strong in-house management and deliberate efforts to recruit and retain an extremely qualified staff and advisors (see Chap. 3). The creative collaboration model, which brings LTIs together with VCs, really only works when the LTIs are proactive and not naive about the GPs' motives; this means LTIs have to have the requisite in-house talent.

2. *External partnerships*: VCs have often failed to keep interests aligned and deliver adequate returns to LPs. Still, VCs' specialized knowledge would be extremely difficult to replicate in-house, which means that VCs still likely have an important role to play. As such, an LTI should develop a handful of deep relationships with VCs to source direct deals in green companies. Moreover, it should consider positioning itself as a 'partner' to VCs rather than as a potential competitor.

3. *Trusted peers*: because it is so hard to build investment capabilities in house, collaborative vehicles that bring direct investors together are also required. As noted above, collaborative vehicles will help long-term investors mobilize the resources and capabilities necessary to pick among the green opportunities ones that are, in fact, commercially viable over the long term. Indeed, syndicating deals among LTIs creates the possibility of tapping into an array of talented people, insight and expertise. And because some of these investments will inevitably fail, pensions and sovereigns could be well served by pooling capital with other, like-minded investors to capture some diversification. The LTIs we studied ran all their in-bound green opportunities through the collaborative team and focused on executing a rigorous and meticulous evaluation of the opportunity.

Conclusions

Venture capital has been out of favour for the past decade or so among the largest institutional investors. Much of this stems from the poor returns generated by external managers because the large majority of VC funds have not outperformed public markets and a majority has failed to even return investee capital. As such, a variety of LTIs have been scaling back their venture capital commitments to external managers and, instead, have been focusing on alternative asset classes that can offer economies of scale, such as private equity, infrastructure and real estate. We argue that venture capital still offers remarkable opportunities for intrepid institutional investors. In our view, the lack of fund performance combined with many company success stories offers a clear opportunity to do something innovative. And that's why we set out to study the asset class and its innovators.

We found a unique opportunity for LTIs to bridge venture-backed, capital-intensive companies to commercial scale and in turn participate in their success over the long term. Rather than seeing a valley of death for these companies, we see a valley of opportunity; the juxtaposition of large past losses coming from green investments with the potential for enormous future gains presents an interesting investment opportunity for long-term investors. And yet, for LTIs to take advantage of this opportunity, they need to re-conceptualize the way they access VC opportunities.

While we believe LTIs have a variety of paths to access these VC opportunities (e.g., in-house teams and seeded managers), we have focused on 'creative collaborations' that bring LPs together with GPs in new, aligned structures. As such, we argue that the time is right for LTIs to launch a new type of venture capital investment platform that can provide direct, diversified, cost-effective and aligned access to quality venture capital opportunities. With this in mind, we presented the case of the Innovation Alliance.

The Innovation Alliance is group of three SWFs that saw an opportunity to use the valley of death to their advantage, extracting investor-friendly terms from companies that could one day disrupt energy markets. The three SWFs also agreed that pooling resources to vet these opportunities was valuable, as venture capital tends to be a highly technical and non-standard asset class. The three peers have made a notional commitment of $1 billion to the alliance and, as of early 2014, have deployed $450 million into green companies.

In the course of our research, we identified several critical success factors for LTIs looking to participate in green ventures. For example, we found that LTIs need to take more responsibility for the deployment of capital, changing the way they view risk and theory. What appeared to be at the core of the success of these vehicles, however, was LTIs not being naive about the relationships they develop to source deals. These 'partnerships' to make capital-intensive investments in VC companies will only work if LTIs have the in-house expertise to vet all of the opportunities that the VCs bring. Thus far, the creative collaborations we saw were functioning effectively. But it is still early days, and the true value of these relationships may not be known for years to come.

7

Does Transparency Restrict Innovation Among Long-term Investors?

Social scientists and policymakers alike have become critical of the pervasive short-termism embedded within finance and its associated markets, institutions and agents. On the one hand, short-termism can be seen as a structural issue that manifests in a number of forms, from the powerful data-engines that offer near-instantaneous views of portfolios to the emphasis many investors place on quarterly and even monthly reporting. In short, the environment in which firms and investors make decisions tends more towards the realization of short-term performance objectives rather than longer-term ones. On the other hand, short-termism can be seen as emanating from cognitive and behavioural biases, where the uncertainty inherent in long-term expectations draws people to shorter rather than longer-term investment horizons.[1] Combining these structural and agential issues brings into question the capacity of investors to price long-term risks or incorporate inter-generational factors into investment decisions.

Sovereign wealth funds (SWFs), however, represent an island of long-term investors in a sea of short-termism. Indeed, a number of commentators have suggested that these funds may be an important source of capital for addressing long-term challenges, while also acting as a counterweight to the issues driving short-termism in global financial markets.[2] Indeed, unlike many institutional investors, most sovereign funds do not possess liabilities

---

[1] George A. Akerlof and Robert J. Shiller, ANIMAL SPIRITS: HOW HUMAN PSYCHOLOGY DRIVES THE ECONOMY, AND WHY IT MATTERS FOR GLOBAL CAPITALISM (Princeton University Press, 2009).

[2] P. Bolton et al., SOVEREIGN WEALTH FUNDS AND LONG-TERM INVESTING (Columbia University Press, 2011).

© The Editor(s) (if applicable) and The Author(s) 2016
J. Singh Bachher et al., *The New Frontier Investors*,
DOI 10.1057/978-1-137-50857-7_7

81

to specific beneficiaries. Moreover, sovereign funds have a single owner, the government sponsor, which, in theory, has a perpetual time horizon.[3] In other words, the rise of sovereign funds may offer creative organizational and institutional designers an opportunity to address the constraints that limit other institutional investors from considering long-term risks alongside more pressing short-term risks.

Notwithstanding sovereign funds' unique characteristics, which provide them with structural foundations conducive to long-term investing and innovation in investment management, they face institutional contradictions at both the international and domestic level. And these contradictions, it seems, can only be reconciled through a public demonstration of short-term performance.[4] Indeed, at the international level there is scepticism regarding the motives underpinning sovereign funds' behaviour, where some worry that they will be used to underwrite mercantilist industrial policies that distort competition and hamper efficiency in product and financial markets.[5] Moreover, there is a fear that these geopolitical motives can be hidden within a sovereign fund's 'long-term investment strategy' by providing these funds with plausible justification for non-commercial (and non-performing) investments. On a domestic level, some sovereign funds also face scepticism as to the justification for saving current government income and investing it outside the home country rather than spending it on goods and services today.[6] This local pressure to 'show results' annually, quarterly or even monthly serves to shrink the investment time horizon of these funds. It may also prevent them from becoming innovative organizations that eschew conventional models of investment management and organizational design.

To counter the scepticism and establish legitimacy, many sovereign funds have been pushed (by their sponsors and domestic and international stakeholders) to prioritize short-term performance, transparency and routine disclosure. This push for greater transparency is at the core of the 'Santiago Principles' (also known as the Generally Accepted Principles and Practices for Sovereign Wealth Funds), which were developed by the International Working Group of SWFs and are now advanced by its successor, the International Forum of

---

[3] We accept that many nation-states are relatively new and the historical geopolitical record would suggest that time horizons for many nation-states are not necessarily perpetual.

[4] Anna Gelpern, *Sovereignty, accountability, and the Wealth Fund Governance Conundrum*, 1 Asian Journal of International Law (2011).

[5] D. Haberly, *Strategic sovereign wealth fund investment and the new alliance capitalism: a network mapping investigation*, 43 Environment and Planning A (2011).

[6] Frederick van der Ploeg and Anthony J. Venables, *Harnessing windfall revenues: optimal policies for resource-rich developing economies*, 121 The Economic Journal (2012).

Sovereign Wealth Funds (IFSWF). The rationale underpinning the Santiago Principles, which were set out in 2008, was to ensure the international legitimacy of these organizations with a view to keeping global financial markets open to sovereign funds. In short, the advanced industrialized economies used the threat of protectionism as a mechanism to force transparency (the presence of symmetric information) on the funds.

The objective of greater transparency is, ultimately, to ensure that the behaviour of sovereign funds remains purely commercial. However, one of the unintended consequences of this focus on transparency and commercial orientation has been to shorten sovereign funds' time horizons. As a result, these theoretically long-term investors are pressed into behaving like the many short-term investors in the marketplace, pushed by structural conditions that demand short-term performance to secure legitimacy (and ensure survival). Said slightly differently, the prerequisite for sovereign funds to secure international and domestic acceptance is to demonstrate performance that matches up to established conventions, which negates the potentially benefits these funds could have in extending the time horizon of 'finance'.

In this chapter, we evaluate the tension that exists between transparency and innovation in the context of long-term investing, using the sovereign fund context to evaluate larger issues relevant to frontier investors, and beneficiary financial institutions more generally. We argue that although a commitment to transparency may drive short-termism, non-transparency is equally harmful to long-term investing because transparency provides a mechanism for examining inefficiencies in the investment process and other malfeasance. Unfortunately, this argument alone is too simplistic and realistically naive. At issue is whether the dichotomy between transparency and non-transparency is this strict and rigid. Even resolutely transparent organizations may find reasons for non-transparency (the presence of asymmetric information) in certain instances, particularly those engaged in a competitive market place or those trying to develop structural advantages in non-competitive markets.

What is needed, we argue, is a more expansive understanding of transparency that separates transparency into different types, such that a more refined conceptual framework for how organizations and their sponsors, in this case sovereign funds, approach and try to resolve the tension between transparency and long-term investing.

The chapter is divided into six parts. In the next section we review the sovereign fund experience and specifically the development and implementation of global transparency standards. In the following section, we discuss how transparency may drive a short-term performance obsession that risks undermining a long-term strategy. This, we argue, may be a reason for the arguably ambiguous record of aggregate sovereign fund transparency, as evidenced in recent IFSWF surveys of Santiago Principles compliance. The following section considers the pros and cons of transparency and the difficulty of communicating a long-term investment strategy to lay audiences. The penultimate section provides a conceptual framework for considering different types of transparency, recognizing the heterogeneity of sovereign funds and sponsors' objectives. The final section concludes.

Threatening the Status Quo?

In 2006, the US government raised concerns over the purchase of UK-based ports operator P&O, which had contracts to run a number of US ports, by DP World, a state-owned company based in the UAE. Although the Committee on Foreign Investment in the United States (CFIUS) approved the deal in 2005, US Coast Guard Intelligence and members of the US Congress brought potential security risks to the fore. Faced with the prospect of a congressional bill to block the deal, DP World voluntarily divested P&O's US operations. DP World's experience (and some would say unfair treatment) was instrumental in the policies that sovereign funds and investment receiving countries would establish when sovereign funds rose to prominence in 2007, as they sought to buy discounted assets associated with the subprime financial crisis.[7]

Having supported the DP World bid as part of an 'open market' foreign policy, the US administration moved to avoid any potential controversy surrounding SWF investments. In the autumn of 2007, at the joint annual meeting of the International Monetary Fund and the World Bank, the US put forth a proposal that sought to maintain and promote openness to SWF investment. The main condition for this access was that SWF investments would have to be demonstrably commercial and eschew political objectives.[8] The IMF took on the task of convening a roundtable of sovereign funds and host countries, known as the International Working Group of SWFs, to identify and draft a set of generally accepted principles and practices (GAPP) that could, in effect, neutralize politicization and ensure a commercial orientation.[9] The idea was to use governance and investment management standards to focus these funds

---

[7] P. Rose, *Sovereign wealth fund investment in the shadow of regulation and politics*, 40 GEORGETOWN JOURNAL OF INTERNATIONAL LAW (2009).

[8] Joseph J. Norton, *The Santiago Principles for Sovereign Wealth Funds: a case study on International Financial Standard-Setting Processes*, 13 JOURNAL OF INTERNATIONAL ECONOMIC LAW (2010).

[9] A. H. B. Monk, *Recasting the sovereign wealth fund debate: trust, legitimacy, and governance*, 14 NEW POLITICAL ECONOMY (2009).

on risk-adjusted financial returns only. The resulting Santiago Principles represent an international effort (led by the advanced OECD economies) to foster more open financial markets with common standards and principles of conduct. In effect, the Santiago Principles are another step in a process of global financial and economic integration, which includes accounting harmonization and increased cooperation among regulators. At the centre of this process is transparency.

Transparency is a fundamental tenet of financial market regulation in the advanced economies. Not only is transparency a requirement for issuers of securities, it is also, in most cases, necessary for the buyers of those securities and the intermediaries in between. For example, in the US, the world's largest capital market, federal regulations require institutional investors to abide by strict disclosure requirements. The Investment Company Act of 1940, which covers mutual funds and other types of professionally managed funds, requires publication of funds' investment policies and periodic reporting of their financial statements. Moreover, the act provides strict guidance as to the composition of directors of the fund and their fiduciary duties. Any changes to the funds' investment policy or its board of directors must occur through a majority vote of the funds' outstanding voting securities.[10] Comparable requirements exist in regulations covering other institutional investors, such as the Employee Retirement Income Security Act of 1974 (ERISA), which covers employer-sponsored private pension plans.[11]

The emphasis on periodic reporting of a fund's financial position and a clearly articulated investment policy is likewise a hallmark of institutional investor regulation in Europe.[12] For example, the 2003 EU Directive on Institutions for Occupational Retirement Provision requires provision of a statement of investment principles as well as regular disclosure of the financial soundness of the fund. Similar measures are likewise found in the EU Directive on Undertakings for Collective Investment in Transferable Securities (UCITS), which covers mutual funds and other collective investment schemes.

Given the regulatory requirements of transparency in institutional investment in advanced economy capital markets, it is unsurprising that the political and regulatory reaction vis-à-vis the emergence of sovereign funds on the world stage was to adopt comparable standards of conduct.[13] Indeed, the

---

[10] Jerry W. Markham, A FINANCIAL HISTORY OF THE UNITED STATES (M.E. Sharpe, 2011).

[11] S. A. Sass, THE PROMISE OF PRIVATE PENSIONS: THE FIRST HUNDRED YEARS (Harvard University Press, 1997).

[12] A. Lamfalussy, *Towards an integrated European financial market*, 24 WORLD ECONOMY (2001).

[13] Edwin M. Truman, SOVEREIGN WEALTH FUNDS: THREAT OR SALVATION? (Peterson Institute for International Economics, 2010).

24 principles governing SWF behaviour in the Santiago agreement evoke the same doctrine of transparency that guides institutional investment in advanced economies. The Santiago Principles are divided into three sections:

- Legal framework, objectives and coordination with macroeconomic policies;
- Institutional framework and governance structure; and
- Investment and risk management framework.

In all three cases, transparency is either evoked directly, through some form of disclosure, or indirectly, through the funds relationship with the sponsoring government. For example, GAPP 1–5, 11–12 and 15–17 directly cite transparency by calling for periodic publication of statistical and financial data and public disclosure of the funds' broader purpose in terms of: its fiscal and macroeconomic policy function and its relationship between the state sponsor; and its investment policy and financial objectives. GAPP 6–10 evoke transparency indirectly by calling for clearly defined standards of conduct and responsibility for the funds' governing body and its operational management, supported by a clearly defined accountability framework.

It is not until GAPP 18 and 19 does a proposition appear that SWF investment decisions should be based on sound portfolio management principles and solely for the purpose of maximizing risk-adjusted financial returns; and, as stated in GAPP 21, that if a SWF exercises its shareholder ownership rights, it should do so only for the purpose of protecting the financial value of its investment. That these three principles appear towards the end, yet encompass many of the primary national security concerns surrounding sovereign funds, is suggestive of the importance of transparency and accountability in bringing sovereign funds in line with other (advanced political economy) institutional investors. It would seem that international legitimacy (and access to global markets) demands disclosure.

But the pressure for disclosure is not simply international: depending on the political authority structure of the SWF, domestic pressure for transparency can be significant as well. For sovereign funds sponsored by developed economy, democratic national or regional governments (e.g. Alberta, Norway, New Zealand, Australia), the pressure for transparency and accountability is usually built into the mandate and operations of the fund. In these cases, the SWF is accountable to parliament, which is accountable to the voters. Given that sovereign funds are ultimately a fiscal resource, they are part and parcel of budgetary politics. Hence, for sovereign funds sponsored by democratic governments, their existence must be justified over competing claims to fiscal resources in relation to social and economic policies. As a result, democratically sponsored sovereign funds must regularly report on their investment objectives and performance with respect to the time-scale of budgetary politics, which can be short in most democracies.

Although the demands for public transparency as a function of legitimacy are to be expected in the case of a representative democracy, the demand for transparency may still be significant in countries with notionally democratic regimes and non-democratic regimes. For example, Singapore's two sovereign funds, Temasek Holdings and the Government of Singapore Investment Corporation (GIC), have become more transparent regarding their respective investment strategies and operations. This is due, on the one hand, to developments globally, but is equally a function of domestic pressure for transparency. Nonetheless, the level of transparency is still limited in comparison with Western funds. For example, the argument proffered by a cabinet minister for the lack of relative transparency of the GIC was to limit the domestic politicization of the fund's global investment strategy.[14]

Transparency and Long-term Investing

As suggested above, the advanced political economies tend to use transparency to understand 'what' and 'how' an organization is doing. Through periodic reporting and disclosure, a stakeholder can examine an organization's strategies and its performance and benchmark this information against competitors to come to some understanding of the relative value of a given organization within the marketplace. Therefore, when it came to writing a governance protocol for sovereign funds that could guarantee commercial behaviour (via the Santiago Principles), these same assumptions (and heuristics) were at the forefront of the designers' thinking. The Santiago Principles make an assumption that if an outsider can understand the 'how' and the 'what' of sovereign funds through regular disclosure, that outsider can derive an insider's understanding of the 'why'; whether sovereign funds were focused on commercial or political goals. By this logic, if SWF performance deviates too much from the conventional 'what' and 'how', the outsider might infer that the behaviour underpinning the investments (the 'why') was something other than commercial, which was (and is) the pressing concern of Western economies faced with the rising prominence of sovereign funds.

---

[14] H. Yeung, *From national development to economic diplomacy? Governing Singapore's sovereign wealth funds*, 24 THE PACIFIC REVIEW (2011).

The problem with this logic is that it ignores the idiosyncrasies and heterogeneity of sovereign funds. These are funds that have differing risk budgets and mandates that make finding benchmarks very challenging. In addition, this heuristic ignores the issue of time (the 'when'). Indeed, the Santiago Principles raise an important question about whether short-term performance is a suitable predictor of long-term performance, as the 'how' benchmark tends to be based on short-term metrics drawn mostly from short-term investors.[15] We think not. Investment decisions that take into consideration both long-term and short-term risks will, at the margin, be different from those investment decisions that seek to maximize short-term performance only. By forcing long-term investors to disclose their performance annually or even quarterly, long-term investors are thus being asked to justify their long-term portfolios in relation to short-term portfolios.

Consider the case of Peru and its private pension funds, which are benchmarked against each other every day. Does a daily return provide an outsider with any information as to the skill of the asset managers over a year? Put another way, if we see one fund with negative performance on a day when another fund has positive performance, is it fair to assume the latter is more commercially viable than the former? Many would agree that daily returns are not a valid predictor of annual returns and should not be used to make judgments of this kind. After all, the investment strategies are probably quite different for the two periods (momentum versus value; technical versus fundamental). In a similar vein, should we rely on quarterly or even yearly returns when assessing the skill (or commercial orientation) of an inter-generational investor? Once again, the investment strategies should be different (public equity versus private equity; financial instruments versus real assets). Is it possible to really understand the 'why' for a long-term inter-generational investor by benchmarking their performance against an investor focused on yearly performance?

Through the Santiago Principles, and their focus on transparency, the advanced political economies are, in effect, attempting to benchmark sovereign funds against conventional investors in the marketplace to ensure commercial and non-threatening behaviour. However, this 'convention' is built around ostensibly short-term institutions (i.e. regulations, norms and conventions) and agents (e.g. market intermediaries and asset managers). To understand the 'why' of sovereign funds, the implied benchmarks for evaluation created by the Santiago Principles should have included the what, how

---

[15] A. Rappaport, *The economics of short-term performance obsession*, 61 FINANCIAL ANALYSTS JOURNAL (2005).

and when. As it stands, the current benchmarks could bias sovereign funds towards shorter-term investments.

This bias towards the short term ostensibly arises from the challenge for the long-term sovereign fund in explaining its operations and plans to a society of lay spectators and their political representatives in such a manner that allows for those spectators to understand and agree to the strategic vision. The difficulty herein lies in the expansive scope and complexity of contemporary financial markets, where expertise and recourse to commonsense investing based on commercial experience and basic levels of education are inadequate. Indeed, in today's markets the breadth of financial products goes well beyond traditional asset classes, as does the different geographies open to investment and their concomitant particularities. As a result, there is a high demand and need for domain-specific knowledge and specialized teams capable of navigating turbulent markets spatially and temporally.[16]

If assembling such capability at a single sovereign fund is a challenge, it is arguably unlikely that the general public (assuming they matter to some degree in the political process in places sponsoring sovereign funds) will have the financial acumen necessary to assess the competency of the fund's managers and the soundness of its strategy, especially when dealing with long time horizons. Simply increasing transparency does not neutralize this problem. For example, in the case of Norway, one of the most transparent funds in the world, it has been argued that it was not the issue of transparency that resulted in public criticism of the SWF in 2008 in the wake of the global financial crisis; it was failing to explain adequately how the fund's strategy and operations could be affected by a crisis.[17] In other words, Norges Bank Investment Management (NBIM) was caught in a 'middle ground' where the general public had enough information to know something had gone wrong but not enough information (or competency) to assess whether the fund was behaving in a competent manner given the circumstances.

While improving the quality of transparency through better explanation and education may deflect criticism of poor performance in the short term, such a strategy still may prove ineffective and be trumped by the salience of and desire for short-term performance metrics. Likewise, domestic opponents of a country's SWF could use the poor performance to reinforce their argument against the existence of the fund or the fund's strategy, assuming that in most cases there is some element of domestic opposition or the pos-

---

[16] Gordon L. Clark, *Expertise and representation in financial institutions: UK legislation on pension fund governance and US regulation of the mutual fund industry*, 2 TWENTY-FIRST CENTURY SOCIETY (2007).

[17] A. Ang et al., *Evaluation of Active Management of the Norwegian Government Pension Fund—Global* at publication year is 2009 https://www0.gsb.columbia.edu/faculty/aang/papers/report%20Norway.pdf

sibility thereof. Hence, the stakes of political interference are still present, which could scuttle even the most basic long-term investment objectives if such interference were to materialize following transitory systemic events. For some sovereign funds in certain places, particularly those without traditions of representative democracy, it may prove easier to limit transparency severely, such as withholding information on asset allocation or even the exact size of the fund. In other words, maintaining a shroud of secrecy and fostering public ignorance has its attractions.

There is thus an argument (which can be heard frequently among SWF stakeholders) for maintaining a certain degree of non-transparency so as to retain the ability to make long-term investments without fear of political repercussions. As a result, it is not surprising to see ambivalence over the disclosure policies in the Santiago Principles from the IFSWF members. While the raw data are unavailable, a report produced by the IFSWF in 2011 based on member surveys provides interesting insights into the tensions surrounding transparency within sovereign funds.[18] According to the report, respondents were asked if they disclosed information on seven elements of investment policy: investment objectives, risk tolerance, investment horizon, strategic asset allocation, investment constraints, leverage and the use of external managers. Of the 21 member funds that responded to the survey, only eight disclosed information on all these elements, despite the fact that all are accepted convention and best practice among institutional investors in advanced markets. Given that the responding funds signed up to the Santiago Principles and joined the IFSWF voluntaril as a way of clarifying their objectives as an institutional investor on global markets, it is surprising to see such levels of (self-reported) non-transparency.

One interpretation for the variability of disclosure is the possible contradictions between a SWF achieving its long-term objectives and maintaining high levels of transparency. The report even states that some members, "argue that certain types of information and the frequency with which it is released might create an overly short-term focus".[19] In other words, the community of sovereign funds is struggling to reconcile the demands for routine transparency and the demands for long-term performance. Given the potential benefits of long-term investing, should the stakeholder community be against this lack of transparency? Or should stakeholders applaud it?

---

[18] See also, S. Bagnall and E. Truman, *IFSWF report on compliance with the Santiago Principles: admirable but flawed transparency*, Peterson Institute for International Economics Policy Brief (2011).

[19] IFSWF Members' Experiences in the Application of the Santiago Principles: Report Prepared by the IFSWF Sub-committee 1 and the Secretariat in Collaboration with the Members of the IFSWF (2011).

Aspects of Transparency

Thus far it may seem as though we are making a case for non-transparency to encourage long-term investment. Undoubtedly, a person or government predisposed to non-transparency would have plenty of fodder for argumentation given the challenges of communicating a complex investment strategy to a lay public. And, considering that the short-termism endemic in global financial markets offers competitive opportunities to those funds that can adopt a long-term approach, it would seem that non-transparency is an acceptable iniquity for protecting a long-term strategy. Furthermore, if we accept that long-term investors can outperform short-term investors over the long run, it would, in turn, suggest that non-transparency offers commercial benefits. All that being said, however, the 'non-transparency short cut' to long-term investing is a risky path, because it means the investor is operating without the consent of society, domestic and international. Moreover, it means trusting the benevolence of the sovereign funds' leaders, whose long-term interests may be individual rather than societal.

Is it possible, then, to produce a situation where a sovereign fund can be both transparent and non-transparent, instead of being either or? Is there a more effective means of fostering greater transparency in aggregate, while allowing for opacity in certain instances, particularly when such opacity justifiably reinforces a long-term strategy and vision? We would contend that revealing acceptable opacity for the preservation of a long-term strategy and vision, whether in the domestic or international domain, could manifest through an enhanced dialogue over the definition(s) of transparency. However, this requires a more systematic clarification of different types of transparency as pertains to sovereign fund operations and governance, which can be used by stakeholders to judge sovereign fund transparency and which, likewise, can be used by sovereign funds and their sponsors in communicating how and in what ways they are transparent.

To this end, we offer a conceptual framework for parsing different types of transparency in the constitution and operation of sovereign funds. Such a framework could be useful for other public long-term investors working to develop innovative models of investment. Taking inspiration from Petra Geraats's conceptual framework for central bank transparency, we distinguish five aspects of sovereign fund transparency: political, procedural, policy, operational and performance.[20] This is illustrated in Table 7.1 with respect to the investment process. Each of these aspects may provide different motives for transparency.

---

[20] Petra M. Geraats, *Central Bank Transparency*, 112 THE ECONOMIC JOURNAL (2002).

Table 7.1 Framing transparency

Transparency domain	Objectives	Methods
Political	To clarify the policy goals of the fund	Mission statement
	To clarify the relationship of the fund to the state	Legal framework
Procedural	To clarify the governance architecture of the fund	Board selection procedure (including requisite qualifications)
		Internal and external delegation procedures
		Corporate engagement procedures
Policy	To clarify the rules and objectives imposed on decision-makers in implementing an investment mandate	Disclosure of investment beliefs and strategic vision
		Corporate engagement policy
Operational	To clarify the way an investment strategy is implemented and by whom	Disclosure of internal and external mandates
		Disclosure of asset allocation, specific investments and intended holding periods
		Corporate engagement actions
Performance	To clarify the investment outcomes achieved by the fund	Short and long-term performance metrics
	To clarify how investment outcomes serve policy goals	External audits
		Qualitative assessment of investment activities
		Qualitative assessment of organizational culture and effectiveness

- *Political transparency* refers to the exogenous rules and regulations under-pinning the fund's operations. Transparency in this domain will clarify the fund's objectives and institutional arrangements as well as the sovereign fund's relationship with the sponsoring government. This could include the sovereign fund's mission statement and the legal framework that defines its existence. Absolute transparency in this domain would also describe the institutional arrangements (formal or otherwise) guiding the interaction between the fund and the government sponsor.
- *Procedural transparency* refers to the resourcing and, indeed, resources at the disposal of the fund to achieve its objectives. Transparency in this domain will generally describe the governance architecture and the decision-making process, both in terms of investments but also in terms of the organizational

requirements. This could include policies for how the board is chosen, arrangements regarding board tenure, and how authority is delegated inside and outside the fund, such as to an investment committee, the selection of external managers and the hiring of staff.

- *Policy transparency* refers to the rules and objectives that the fund—generally through its formal governance arrangements—imposes on its own operations and personnel. Transparency in this domain will thus highlight the fund's strategic vision, investment, beliefs and strategy. This could include information about asset allocation, geographic distribution of investments and risk budgeting.
- *Operational transparency* refers to the way the investment strategy is implemented and by whom. Transparency in this domain will describe the ways in which the fund seeks to put policies into action, such as how the fund plans to access financial markets, certain industries, geographies or even specific assets. This could include information on whether assets are managed in-house or through external asset managers, and what type of involvement the fund has with the investee entities in which the fund invests.
- *Performance transparency* refers to the investment outcomes achieved by the fund. Such transparency could be quantitative performance and judged against appropriate peers or, more often, bespoke benchmarks that reflect the fund's risk-return profile. Transparency could also be qualitative and judged through external and independent audits of subjective criteria that focus on a specific organizational culture.

For some, these may invoke underlying principles from the Santiago regime and many of the national regulatory frameworks facing sovereign funds when investing internationally. To this we would not disagree, save for transparency related to performance. For some funds it may be possible to be completely transparent to a significant degree across all these domains. But even these funds, as highlighted in the case of New Zealand in the next section, would still require complementary mechanisms to manage potential criticisms, particularly related to short-term performance. But for other sovereign funds, limiting transparency across some of these domains may be more appropriate. However, just as the fully transparent fund requires complementary mechanisms for managing the outcomes of its transparency, the fund that is opaque will need to justify such asymmetric information.

Importantly, though, the fund and/or its sponsor may justify opacity in one area, such as performance, by pointing to robust transparency in other areas. In other words, the fund may be able to demonstrate the 'what' and the 'why', as required for international and possibly domestic legitimacy, without having to reveal the 'how' and 'when' in the short term. Hence, the fund could be said to be transparent in the context of performance, but it may offer a distinct timeline on which performance is revealed.

Two Views of Transparency

Contrary to the view that transparency may harm a long-term strategy, the New Zealand Superannuation Fund (NZSF) demonstrates that transparency is not antithetical to a long-term approach. Indeed, the NZSF, which routinely tops the list of the most transparent funds, is the only sovereign fund we are aware of that is required by law to publish monthly performance figures. Considering that the asset allocation is weighted heavily towards equities, which are volatile in the short run, and towards atypical and illiquid investment options, which require a long-term commitment to realize their potential, the fund is at a higher risk of facing criticism during periods of market uncertainty and following major market events. As a result, it has had to prioritize effective communication, through pro-active disclosure and outreach, as a core competency of the fund. Accordingly, remarkable detail is provided on how funds are invested. For example, the NZSF details how it tries to generate alpha (beat the markets); when and how it uses derivatives; how environmental social and governance considerations are incorporated into operations and investments; when the fund chooses to invest its assets in-house; and what it looks for in its third-party asset managers.[21]

While the NZSF appears to have squared the equation between long-term investing and high transparency, political reality would suggest that it is unlikely to become standard across most sovereign funds. This is certainly disappointing for proponents of high levels of transparency, but is the New Zealand approach, which is common to many of the sovereign funds from democratic countries, the only means of reconciling the transparency/long-term investing conundrum?

We mentioned earlier that the Government of Singapore Investment Corporation (GIC) has become more transparent since 2008, specifically regarding its governance, investment strategy and global operations. This is due, on the one hand, to developments globally, but it is equally a function of domestic pressure when the government had to withdraw funds to support the economy in the wake of the global economic downturn of 2007–2008. In terms of the 'when', the GIC emphasizes disclosure of its real returns on

---

[21] See www.nzsuperfund.co.nz/how-we-invest [last accessed 15 October 2015].

time scales of five, 10 and 20 years. As such, the GIC is being transparent regarding its performance, but in the form of smoothed performance metrics over the long term in place of volatile short-term performance metrics in the short term. In other words, the GIC is trying to demonstrate the 'what' and the 'how', as required for international and possibly domestic legitimacy, without revealing the short-term 'how'. Hence, the fund could be said to be transparent in the context of performance, but it may offer a distinct timeline on which performance is revealed.

Conclusions

This book makes the case that long-term institutional investors have a strategic advantage that they are often not leveraging in their investment strategy. In fact, as we argue in this chapter, much of the regulatory and governance frameworks make it hard for long-term investors to behave in a long-term way. Specifically, we argue that transparency and long-term investing are beneficial for society, but there is often a tension between the two. Too much transparency may seem for some counterproductive to long-term investing, as it may drive short-termism. Conversely, rationing transparency is counter to obtaining society's acquiescence, which is a fundamental concern in democratic states and one of the demands of the international community and a norm of contemporary financial markets. This much is clear in the framing of the Santiago Principles. In effect, no large investor can avoid calls for greater transparency if it wants unfettered access to global markets and domestic commitment for their organization. As such, the competition between transparency and long-term investing tends to be won by transparency. But, in our view, this competition can be won by both phenomena, as the New Zealand case demonstrates.

Yet, there is a larger significance to our argument. If there is an impetus to 'remake finance' in the wake of the 2008–2009 financial crisis, it is necessary, therefore, that scholars, institutional designers and those ultimately managing the assets think critically about how to build a long-term investor that is sufficiently resourced in terms of set-up and human resources to overcome the variables, structural and behavioural, that drive short-termism in global financial markets. Whereas regulation may curb some of the excesses of exuberance-prone markets, it is equally important that such regulatory reform, however effective, be buttressed by reform at the organizational level as well as through better governance architecture and processes. Without concomitant reformulation of the way the institutions at the centre of global financial markets operate and govern the ways they invest and engage opportunities in the real economy, regulation will be circumscribed by regulatory arbitrage and policy drift over time.

But fixing the inside of the organization does not go far enough in resisting the forces of short-termism. As the NZSF demonstrates, public dialogue is as important as being at the leading edge of global financial markets. Saving for the future requires a perpetual dialogue with the public as to why and how the sovereign fund fits with the long-term social contract, and what needs to be done for it to meet such an obligation. Indeed, the long-term fund cannot use short-term returns as a metric for evaluating the ability of its managers, as quarterly performance is not a useful indicator of decennial performance. In other words, a long-term investor may actually need to be more articulate, more transparent and more accountable (at least within its stakeholder community) than a short-term fund that has the luxury of pointing to its short-term returns as an indicator of ability or competency. Moreover, perpetual communication is important, as no political regime lasts forever. Democracies hold regular elections and dictators are deposed or die. Yet, this does not mean that a country's sovereign wealth need succumb to that change as well. As the case of Libya shows, even though the Gaddafi dynasty has been removed the new government has been working to reform the governance of the Libyan Investment Authority.[22] Hence, we should be optimistic that sovereign funds can outlive the political cycle and fulfil long-term goals for society.

The broader story here for long-term investors is that being innovative can be challenging when stakeholders and the general public can watch and potentially scrutinize every move you make. This is no excuse not to be innovative. In some places such scrutiny does not happen, or at least not so publicly. And let's not forget that scrutiny is useful, providing a check on whether decisions are sound and not some overambitious vanity project. If successful organizations are learning organizations, they should also communicate and educate their stakeholders on how they are to achieve their goals over the long term. It is about continuously articulating a vision of the future and what is possible.

---

[22] See Sven Behrendt and Rachel Ziemba 'Libyan Investment Authority. What's Next?' www.economonitor.com/blog/2011/08/libyan-investment-authority-whats-next/ [accessed 15 October 2015].

8

Catalyzing Development in a Short-term World

Thus far, our narrative has focused on beneficiary investors in middle to high-income economies. This is a simple function of where wealth is concentrated, and thus where a greater proportion of large beneficiary financial institutions are located. We would be myopic, however, if we did not include a discussion of potential frontier investors in the developing world. Many developing economies have made big strides in development and are becoming integrated with global financial markets. Indeed, frontier investors from the rich world continue to see growth opportunities and opportunities for collaboration in emerging markets, not least because of their comparatively young populations. And, many developing countries have recently established or intend to establish a sovereign fund. But including consideration of investors in developing economies also helps to reinforce the view that, ultimately, finance and investment should be about developing the real economy.

Sovereign wealth funds may be a vital component of a country's economic development strategy, particularly in low and middle-income, resource-rich countries.[1] In theory, sponsoring governments can wield an investment fund to fulfil policy objectives, such as smoothing the volatility of resource revenues to support government spending over time, managing currency appreciation, developing local economic capacity, financing social services (e.g. health and education), reducing the sovereign risk profile in global capital markets, facilitating inter-generational wealth transfers, and as a tool for restricting the misappropriation and misallocation of state resources. Given this potential,

---

[1] Udaibir S. Das et al., ECONOMICS OF SOVEREIGN WEALTH FUNDS: ISSUES FOR POLICYMAKERS (International Monetary Fund, 2010).

J. Singh Bachher et al., *The New Frontier Investors*,
DOI 10.1057/978-1-137-50857-7_8

many governments are considering or are already setting up state-sponsored investment institutions. This is particularly the case in sub-Saharan Africa.

Although estimates vary, the number of funds in sub-Saharan Africa that meet the International Monetary Fund's definition of a sovereign fund range from the low- to mid-teens; with sponsors from Angola and Botswana to Ghana and Nigeria. Add to that the number of countries considering or constructing sovereign funds, and sub-Saharan Africa could soon be home to upwards of 20 sovereign funds.[2] It has been suggested that sovereign funds in low-income countries should be cast—and indeed some inherently are—as sovereign development funds (SDF).[3] SDFs are a type of sovereign fund, with specific development-related aims and investment mandates. With this rush to build institutions, there is an underlying optimism that these investment funds could bring benefits in terms of economic growth and development for sponsoring countries.

Notwithstanding their potential usefulness in the policy toolkit, state-sponsored investment funds are not a panacea for the challenges facing resource-rich countries in sub-Saharan Africa and elsewhere.[4] Indeed, while a special-purpose investment vehicle may provide some optimism to the resource wealthy, it is not a replacement for broader institutional development.[5] A state-sponsored investment fund does not replace the need to foster and stimulate a capable and active workforce; nor does it replace effective regulation and the rule of law. The creation of a state-sponsored investment fund will not, on its own, improve fiscal and monetary outcomes.[6] Some countries may unwisely move towards establishing a sovereign fund before thinking through the many other ways to encourage economic development.[7] Likewise, there are other strategies for employing resource wealth to develop an economy, many of which do not require a state-sponsored institutional investor.[8]

---

[2] V. Barbary et al., *The new investment frontier: SWF investment in Africa*, in BRAVING THE NEW WORLD: SOVEREIGN WEALTH FUND INVESTMENT IN THE UNCERTAIN TIMES OF 2010 (V. Barbary & B. Bortolotti, eds., 2011).

[3] J. Santiso, *Sovereign development funds: key actors in the shifting wealth of nations*, 9 REVUE D'ÉCONOMIE FINACIÈRE (2009).

[4] R. M. Auty, RESOURCE ABUNDANCE AND ECONOMIC DEVELOPMENT (Oxford University Press, 2001); M. L. Ross, THE OIL CURSE: HOW PETROLEUM WEALTH SHAPES THE DEVELOPMENT OF NATIONS (Princeton University Press, 2012).

[5] Daron Acemoglu and James A. Robinson, WHY NATIONS FAIL: THE ORIGINS OF POWER, PROSPERITY AND POVERTY (Crown Publishers, 1st ed., 2012).

[6] Jeffrey M. Davis et al., FISCAL POLICY FORMULATION AND IMPLEMENTATION IN OIL-PRODUCING COUNTRIES (International Monetary Fund, 2003).

[7] Paul Collier et al., *Managing resource revenues in developing economies*, 57 IMF STAFF PAPERS (2010).

[8] T. Gylfason, *Natural resource endowment: a mixed blessing?*, CESIFO WORKING PAPER SERIES (2011).

Such optimism for the potential of sovereign funds in resource-revenue management should be tempered because implementing and sustaining a sovereign fund 'solution' to the resource curse is inherently complex. On the one hand, governing, managing and operating a sovereign fund poses organizational and geographical challenges, such as attracting and retaining capable investment managers and accessing attractive deal flows, as we have discussed in previous chapters. Simply maintaining a long-term, risk-adjusted rate of return on global markets requires a form and function akin to other professionalized investment organizations. Moreover, a particular set of governance principles needs to be met, and the fund needs to be able to operate with a degree of relative autonomy under professionalized conditions, such that it is insulated from partisan politics and bureaucratic encroachment. This does not mean, however, that the sponsoring political authority does not set the mandate and higher-level principles of the sovereign fund. What this suggests, ultimately, is that for the sovereign fund, or more specifically the SDF, to encourage development, it must be purpose-built to meet financial and commercial objectives.

Defining what that purpose should be and what is possible is, however, complicated by several factors. On the one hand, the form of government of the sovereign sponsor and the significance of public legitimacy may help or hinder investment mandates. To be more precise, certain investment mandates may be more easily implemented and sustained by different forms of government, notwithstanding the long-term implications for economic growth and development that different forms of government bring. On the other hand, different investment mandates (e.g. direct private equity investment against passive diversified portfolio investment in public markets) and their relative sophistication require organizational capabilities and expertise that are probably not available locally or are insufficiently developed, such that the implementation of certain investment mandates is constrained and/or too costly. Ultimately, then, the purpose and the possibilities of a state-sponsored investment fund depend on local conditions. What works for one country may not be suitable for another.

In this chapter we provide a sympathetic critique of SDFs—an expanding group of frontier investors. As such, we unpack the scope and possibilities of SDFs in different forms and under different political-*cum*-institutional conditions as a policy tool supporting economic growth and development, but without overstating their potential or playing down the constraints that limit their effectiveness. The argument is developed as follows. The next section considers the potential of SDFs in meeting policy objectives supportive of economic growth and development. We then describe two ideal types of

SDFs, focusing on the organizational demands and constraints that arise from different organizational aims and investment objectives, while addressing the potential constraints facing different types of SDF in relation to politics. The penultimate section sets out some principles and policies to consider in the design of a strategic investment fund on the frontiers of finance.

Sovereign Fund Solutions

What role could a sovereign fund can play in supporting sustainable economic growth and development over the long term? Although SDFs are not exclusive to resource-rich countries, much of the current development of these institutions occurs in these countries. At issue for resource-rich countries is how to manage and spend resource revenue over time, and by which means. Let us make clear here that in considering SDFs, our argument is not that these financial institutions become a replacement for conventional forms of fiscal governance, where the decisions on how to use resource revenues are made by an accountable authority (e.g. parliament). An SDF is a policy tool, not a replacement for wider institutional development. They are, ultimately, financial institutions with limited capabilities for confronting wider issues related to economic growth and development, which must include other fit-for-purpose policies and institutions.

Macroeconomic Stability

As resource revenues are an important part of the government budget for resource-rich countries, it is necessary to ensure some degree of stability. These revenues have to support long-term planning and it is important to avoid socioeconomic distress if spending has to be cut for a short period, knowing that commodity prices can be volatile from one year to the next. It is an issue of ensuring macroeconomic and financial stability in the wider economy, particularly if that economy is dependent on government spending and economic activity associated with natural resource production. On these grounds, the creation of a stabilization fund, a type of sovereign wealth fund, takes precedent over the creation of an SDF that has more targeted objectives. In that respect, a stabilization fund takes a passive role in economic growth and development. In that case and although very important to economic growth and development, we would not classify a stabilization fund as an SDF.

A stabilization fund smoothes commodity price volatility by setting aside a portion of the revenue during periods of high prices so that the government has a stable source of income during periods of low prices. Such stability is important as it helps stretch the planning and investment time horizon of the state, particularly if the state is devoted to supporting the diversification of the economy and the productivity of the workforce in other areas. As financial institutions, stabilization funds, which in many countries are incorporated into the central bank, are short-term-oriented and intolerant of risk. They hold cash and a variety of liquid assets (namely US Treasuries) that can be quickly mobilized should the government have a need for them. The assets are normally held in foreign-denominated assets to minimize appreciation of the local currency and to help manage the capacity of the economy to absorb the inflationary effects of a booming extractive sector. In other words, the stabilization fund slows the appreciation of the real exchange rate, which would otherwise harm development—a phenomenon sometimes referred to as 'Dutch disease'.

Knowing that markets are prone to crisis and that economies experience macroeconomic shocks of various sorts, such as a local banking crisis or an international balance-of-payments crisis, a stabilization fund can function as a lender of last resort that acts as a buffers against the worst of these crises and their long-term effects. One partial reason many countries have established a stabilization fund is to limit the need to access external help in the event of a shock, as such external intervention comes with conditions that may be overly harsh, potentially unsuitable for local conditions, and politically undesirable. Some East Asian countries established SWFs in the form of foreign-exchange reserves and budget surpluses because of their experience with International Monetary Fund structural adjustment policies following the Asian financial crisis of 1997.[9]

In reality, then, an SDF is of secondary or even tertiary importance in managing resource revenues and using those revenues directly for economic development. Put differently, in the institutional chain of resource revenue management, the SDF comes after a stabilization fund, which exists as a supplement of the government budget, providing stability to resource revenues. This begs the question as to when the creation of an SDF is appropriate and for what purposes. Although this suggests that the SDF is ill-suited to supporting macroeconomic and financial stability, a task more appropriate to a stabilization fund, the SDF may play a role in supporting productive efficiency and distributive justice.

---

[9] S. Griffith-Jones and J. A. Ocampo, *The rationale for sovereign wealth funds: a developing country perspective, in* SOVEREIGN WEALTH FUNDS AND LONG-TERM INVESTING (P. Bolton et al. eds., 2011).

Productive Efficiency

There are two ways that an SDF can aid efforts to improve the productive efficiency of the economy: making strategic investments; and contributing to the development of local financial market capacity. In the first instance, an SDF can be thought of as a plug-in to global markets, where the SDF is used to make strategic alliances with firms and other foreign investors. In the process, the SDF can facilitate technology and knowledge transfer, which helps raise the productive capability of local industry, thus increasing the potential returns on local assets. However, noting the importance of broader institutional development, such investments would need to coincide with social and education policies that improve skills and workforce participation. Put simply, the SDF is an additional policy tool supplementing wider policy efforts. By supporting industrial policy, an SDF can therefore encourage diversification of the economy. As experience shows, the shift from primary commodity production to industrial and services production generally coincides with higher growth rates.[10] This practice is employed by SDFs in Gulf states, as governments there press to diversify their economies away from their dependence on hydrocarbon production.[11]

In the second instance, if foreign investors are reluctant to invest in untried and underdeveloped markets, the SDF can be the necessary element that helps attract investment from both local and foreign sources. By helping foment capital market development and market liquidity locally, which may coincide with strategic alliances made internationally or co-investment with other institutional investors from elsewhere, the SDF could help improve the investment climate over time. The SDF sits as the translator between the local government and the international community, with latter bringing credibility by confirming an investment's commercial motivations and viability. Nonetheless, this also requires that such investment be coupled with prudential regulation and enforcement.

The best-performing and well-managed SDFs in more developed economies behave more like wealth creators than wealth appreciators. A wealth creation strategy is exemplified by private agents helping to act as a catalyst for enterprises or projects, such as is the case for private equity, infrastructure and real estate developers or high-risk, high-reward venture capital (VC). These

---

[10] Angus Maddison, THE WORLD ECONOMY: A MILLENNIAL PERSPECTIVE (Development Centre of the Organisation for Economic Co-operation and Development, 2001).

[11] D. Haberly, *Strategic sovereign wealth fund investment and the new alliance capitalism: a network mapping investigation*, 43 ENVIRONMENT AND PLANNING A (2011).

investors tend to take relatively large, direct, strategic stakes in projects. By using their internal capabilities and resources in conjunction with selected partners, these types of investors seek higher returns on their holdings. Wealth creators also 'manage' returns by involving themselves in the operations of their investments, taking, for example, board-level positions so as to provide governance and management scrutiny. Compared with a portfolio approach, a 'wealth creating' strategy necessitates large stakes in a concentrated set of investments for which the investor can add value over the long run and, as such, engender more sustainable and, indeed, superior-market returns.

Most successful SDFs in more developed economies function in a way similar to private market funds and partnerships. SDFs differ from private market agents and other long-term investors on a fundamental level: these institutions are driven by a mandate to generate financial returns from their investments *and* contribute to a country's or region's economic development. In this manner, SDFs are required to deliver on two—or "double"—bottom lines: the first bottom line is to generate financial returns consistent with expectations, and the second bottom line is to drive national economic development policy through their investments. These imperatives are normally expressed in legal, governance and management frameworks. Where SDFs operate as wealth creators, participating in the economic development of their countries through the direct acquisition and growth of national assets, their operations are designed to match their ambitions.

Given that the best SDFs are strategic and tactical investors driven by the imperative to create wealth, it is clear that to do so relies on more than conventional portfolio management tools. Indeed, the best SDFs leverage what is called "structural alpha". While conventional wisdom holds that the best performing VC firms benefit from exceptional staff and cutting-edge knowledge, this alone cannot wholly account for their long-term success. The best VCs benefit from structural advantages that are developed over time: small differences in investment capabilities and resources produce cumulative advantages that are meaningful over time. These advantages come from the identification of, and capitalization on, 'positive feedback control loops' that reinforce hegemony in relation to other firms. In other words, private investors cultivate sources of private information that they alone are able to exploit over the longer term.

In the same way that the most successful VC and private equity (PE) investors are adept at capturing structural alpha, so too are the best SDFs. For instance, the top SDFs identify, capitalize on, and lock-in local knowledge of their markets, domestic industries, and macro-economic trajectories so as to realize more sophisticated and precise estimations of long-term returns. This is especially important when a sovereign fund operates as a wealth creator rather than a wealth appreciator. Similarly, internal control of the investment process, typical of the best SDFs given the markets they tend to operate in are nascent and starved of capital, allows a reordering of the relationships between sovereigns and their service providers and co-investors. With the power to set terms for the flow of commitments and flow of returns over different durations, SDFs can manage the relationships and alignment between global investment institutions. In turn, this generates stronger relationships and greater opportunities to make deals with aligned parties. Moreover, local investing, patient investing, and control over the investment process can enable collateral or 'synergetic' returns, such as property development projects around infrastructure investments.[12] This is especially important in circumstances where development is clustered in nodes of innovation and human capital, wherein an investor can sustain superior investment rates of return through the positive externalities of development.

In light of these examples of the kinds of structural alpha that SDFs can leverage, we have devised a matrix for categorizing these funds by objectives and links to national endowments and advantages. Figure 8.1 suggests ways in which SDFs can operate in terms of improving productive capacity.

In Fig. 8.1, the matrix places SDFs on two axes.[13] The horizontal axis ranges from 'strategic' to 'commercial', in terms of investment objectives. Note that commercial entities need not outperform strategic entities; rather it is simply a function of whether the market is setting the agenda or the government. Since SDFs are strategic and/or tactical investors, funds harness their portfolio or acquire structural assets so as to improve their performance and benefit from the financial upside of industrial development. Alternatively, SDFs may identify and capitalize on emerging opportunities in promising industries, thereby attracting private and public capital to accelerate development. In turn, we juxtapose the investment objectives axis against SDFs' links to national endowments and advantages, in terms of how loosely or how tightly coupled the SDF is to the national assets. For instance, this reflects the evolution of Malaysia's Khazanah where the fund shifted from holding a large portion of structural national assets, to developing local enterprises. In effect, the fund has partially privatized its holdings.

---

[12] A single investment in a single asset may not pencil in terms of IRR, but if that investment also serves as a catalyst for a new ecosystem from which many opportunities arise, the SDF can be well positioned for outperformance.

[13] Here we take inspiration from Henry W. Chesbrough, *Making sense of corporate venture capital*, 80 HARVARD BUSINESS REVIEW (2002).

OPERATIVE OBJECTIVES

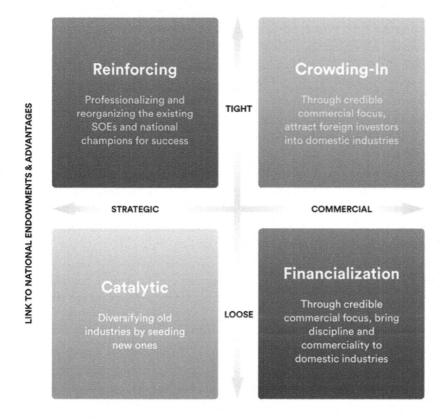

Fig. 8.1   Sovereign development fund strategies

Within these two axes, the ways in which SDFs operate to optimize performance are positioned. Although these investment operations are arranged in distinct components, this does not mean to say an SDF need adopt just one strategy. Indeed, the best SDFs can and do adopt a variety of these strategies to maximize developmental and financial returns. The four operational strategies are:

- *Reinforcing*: for SDFs in possession of underperforming national assets, be it companies, infrastructure, or other real assets, are responsible for reorganizing, professionalizing and encouraging innovatation in their holdings so as to drive development and higher returns.
- *Attracting investment*: SDFs participating in emerging domestic industries reap greater financial and developmental returns when private and public

capital (of other nations) also commit capital to those industries. For example, if SDFs can credibly display commercial acumen, they can syndicate local deals with investors that might have sought opportunities elsewhere.

• *Catalytic*: SDFs that are less tied to particular industries or the endowed national assets can act as a catalyst for new industries, thereby diversifying the economy away from industries that are either no longer profitable or sustainable over the long-term. These SDFs can also help fill 'white space' in an economy by providing answers to (and investments around) the question, What's missing from this ecosystem that will undoubtedly be here in ten years?

• *Financialization*: by virtue of their capabilities and resources, SDFs can deepen the financial infrastructure of the local economy, thereby underwriting the development process simply through the growth of the capital market and the emergence of financial intermediaries and investors focused on opportunities in the region.

Countries considering SDFs do so for varying economic and developmental objectives, so the operations will vary one from the other. Beyond the taxonomy presented above, the performance of SDFs is dependent on how effective they are in executing their operations.

The most successful SDFs adopt long-term, patient investor strategies integrating environmental, social and governance factors with their investment operations. Whether streamlining existing holdings or acquiring assets to enhance performance, SDFs typically use operational structures that look like private equity buyout shops, complete with partners. Other successful SDFs are those that have the mandate to launch or 'seed' new industries, with the view to participating alongside acquired companies in these industries. The best SDFs identify synergetic and complementary industries around emerging companies, thereby accelerating development.

Distributive Justice

Many resource-rich countries and developing countries face challenges with poverty and inequality. In many cases this is due to corruption that has been sustained by the resource wealth itself. Assuming that the sovereign sponsor seeks some degree of public legitimacy in relation to the establishment and long-term success of an SDF, there are a number of ways an SDF could be used to solidify its legitimacy while contributing to distributive justice and poverty alleviation. Again, we should emphasize that the SDF is not a replacement for other institutional reforms and social policies that reduce poverty and inequality.

Whereas the population of most developing countries is relatively young and the income and wealth of households is low, a system of cash transfers could be set up whereby a portion of the investment returns of the fund are directly distributed to the public.[14] The point here is to ensure collective equity. On the one hand, this may help raise individual purchasing power and the ability of households and individuals to plan for the future, such as investing in skills. On the other hand, by giving the public a direct stake in the success of the fund, there may be an increased probability that the public will demand greater transparency and accountability such that those managing the fund and/or those that are directing the managers of the fund, the sovereign sponsors, are less likely to misappropriate funds and/or misallocate funds to politically-motivated projects.

If Dutch disease and consumption-led inflation are severe problems or potentially severe problems, individual citizens could be given individual accounts tied to the returns of the SDF. However, these accounts cannot be tapped until a person reaches a certain age, which mitigates the speed and degree at which funds are repatriated for local consumption. As such, individual citizens become stakeholders in the fund's long-term success. They also see the direct benefits of the fund much like cash transfers would, but at a later period.

A Basic Typology

Two types of development fund can be identified. The first, or Type I, is a fund that is an actively managed fund akin to a private equity or venture capital fund that makes domestic and potentially foreign investments. Obviously, we would not rule out public equities, but as suggested previously there is some debate as to the degree that stock markets spur development in low-income economies, particularly in the absence of effective supervisory capabilities. As supervision improves, it is foreseeable that public markets will be used to divest mature holdings (this mirrors the model of Singapore's Temasek

---

[14] See, T. Moss, *Oil to cash: fighting the resource curse through cash transfers* Center for Global Development Working Papers *at* www.cgdev.org/files/1424714_file_Oil2Cash_primer_FINAL.pdf. If, on the other hand, a country is undergoing relatively rapid demographic ageing, wherein such ageing will constrain economic growth and fiscal resources in the future, the SDF could be used to support intergenerational saving. But this is not the case for most developing countries, particularly in sub-Saharan Africa. Nonetheless, the SDF in the context of demographic aging can be used to cover shortfalls in the public pension system, thus ensuring intergenerational equity.

or Malaysia's Khazanah). To reiterate, a Type I SDF is focused on facilitating the economy's productive potential through proactive investments that seek to catalyze industries. One can also include infrastructure investments under this type as well.

The second type of SDF, or Type II, is a fund that invests in a global portfolio that could return a cash dividend to all citizens (comparable to the Alaska Permanent Fund, for example), or a cash flow that can be used to support other development-related spending (e.g. health and education). In addition to helping mitigate Dutch disease, the cash dividend is about boosting the purchasing power of the poor. And, again, it is important to remember how poor the average citizen of a developing country is. Ultimately, a Type II sovereign development fund is about distributive justice. In short, the two types have different goals and they have different investment styles. As such, there are different demands on these organizations as financial institutions. Understanding their constraints as financial institutions provides further insight into their viability in certain contexts, and therefore their suitability as a policy tool.

People and Organizational Design

To achieve any objective, a sovereign fund requires a governance structure that is appropriate to its capabilities and the size of assets under management. But, effective governance can come in many forms that account for inherited constraints and local conditions. What works for Singapore or Abu Dhabi may not be appropriate for what can work in Ghana or Mozambique. Local inputs can vary widely. Successful institutional investors require employees with the necessary skills, competencies and experience to manage a modern financial institution. This task can be challenging for SDFs because they are public organizations investing in private markets. As such, they must find ways to fill public sector jobs with people who can compete in and with the private sector. Successful institutional investors require, moreover, highly developed decision-making frameworks and risk mitigation capabilities to manage the complexities of investing across global financial markets or investing in private assets where due diligence is critical. Ultimately, the skills of the staff should dictate the level risk taken by the fund and the assets and geographies that the fund invests in.

Insourcing asset management is not an option for most small SDFs, at least initially. Insourcing is a challenge even for organizations in advanced economies where local capabilities are likely to be much larger and more developed.[15] Ultimately, to mimic the market for financial services internally within the organization is not without considerable challenges. Doing so may generate, on the one hand, issues of size and expertise. Often only the very largest funds are perhaps financially capable of enveloping most functions. Yet, large organizations may struggle with complexity and organizational inertia that limits flexibility in the face of changing conditions. On the other hand, where organizations exist in an environment without rivals or comparable organizations, there is a risk of organizational deterioration and complacency.[16] This is a situation some SDFs may find themselves in domestically, limiting the scope for inter-organizational knowledge transfers and for benchmarking through competition. Coupled with the challenge of how to govern effectively a range of functions, bringing more and more of the 'market' within the organization is risky.

In both cases, however, delegation of the investment mandate is possible in theory. But for a Type I SDF, viability depends on the availability of local skills and expertise. Delegation does not necessarily solve this problem. While some developing countries certainly have local capabilities in this area, for many it is unlikely to be available, rendering the Type I option less attractive. Clearly, delegation to third-party asset managers is much easier for a Type II SDF, which solves the expertise problem. While costs may be an issue, there is no shortage of large assets managers in New York and London or other regional and international financial centres that can provide global portfolio management services.

In that respect, a Type II SDF at country-level consists of a board (and potentially an investment committee) that meets to decide on asset allocation and reviews managers. The other significant task is administering the dividends, which itself comes with problems in poor countries as financial exclusion would constrain the ability to distribute funds to those most in need, or the administration of long-term savings accounts.[17] But new technologies have started to provide banking services to the poor, such as M-Pesa in Kenya.[18] Such constraints may limit the viability of a dividend system, suggesting that proceeds may be better suited to financing other development-related needs (e.g. public health).

---

[15] Gordon L. Clark and Ashby H. B. Monk, *The scope of financial institutions: in-sourcing, outsourcing and off-shoring*, 13 JOURNAL OF ECONOMIC GEOGRAPHY (2013).

[16] A counterargument is that such organizational isolation could allow for innovation and a long-term approach because there is less pressure to mimic peers and to succumb to herd behaviour.

[17] Beatriz Armendariz and Jonathan Morduch, THE ECONOMICS OF MICROFINANCE (MIT Press, 2nd ed. 2010).

[18] Jenny C. Aker and Isaac M. Mbiti, *Mobile phones and economic development in Africa*, 24 THE JOURNAL OF ECONOMIC PERSPECTIVES (2010).

Two Views of Finance

The difference in investment style between Type I and Type II brings up another issue that requires consideration. That finance and the financial system are an important component of any market economy is not a question of debate. Even so, the debate is not settled regarding at what point in developing a productive market economy that finance and the financial system enter. For some, finance leads development. For others, finance follows development.[19] The former point of view, which is often attributed to the ideas of Joseph Schumpeter, contends that financial intermediaries, such as a Type I SDF, identify and finance entrepreneurs and technological changes that lead to economic growth and development.[20] Accordingly, the sophistication and quality of financial institutions and the financial services industry as a real sector is critical. Financial intermediaries emerge in advance of the demand for their services, assets, and liabilities. Individual financial institutions and the industry as a whole play a role in economic growth and change, identifying, researching and financing the most promising sectors, firms, corporate managers and entrepreneurs. This view assumes, in effect, that finance is supply-leading.

The latter point of view, often associated with the ideas of post-Keynesian economist Joan Robinson, contends that the financial system follows in the wake of enterprising firms, providing a conduit through which savings can be transferred from slow-growth sectors to high-growth sectors.[21] Put simply, the financial system is responsive to the demand for its services. As entrepreneurs and firms identify opportunities that cannot be financed with their own internal resources, the financial system responds by providing services and capital to see these opportunities to completion. Compared with the supply-leading view, this demand-following view sees a much less important role for the financial services industry as a real sector. It is much less critical to the growth and development process. Financial institutions are passive actors.

Subscribing to this demand-following view, one would be unlikely to see any benefit in establishing a Type I SDF. A Type II fund, in contrast, adheres to this logic. In reality, financial systems are likely to have elements of supply-leading and demand-following finance. Some financial intermediaries may engender entrepreneurial development at small and industrial scales. Other

---

[19] H. Patrick, *Financial development and economic growth in underdeveloped countries*, 14 ECONOMIC DEVELOPMENT AND CULTURAL CHANGE (1966).

[20] J. Schumpeter, THE THEORY OF ECONOMIC DEVELOPMENT: AN INQUIRY INTO PROFITS, CAPITAL, CREDIT, INTEREST, AND THE BUSINESS CYCLE (Harvard University Press, 1934).

[21] J. Robinson, THE RATE OF INTEREST, AND OTHER ESSAYS (Macmillan, 1952).

financial intermediaries may simply fulfil the demands brought by enterprising firms. For a developing economy, the decision to develop either type of SDF may rest on the balance between the two forms of finance. But even in the supply-leading view, financial intermediaries can be very wrong sometimes. Skilled staff and organizational design, as discussed above, matter greatly. For every consistently successful venture capital or private equity firm, there are many mediocre ones. Even if the supply-leading view has a certain appeal, as it allows for specific, focused investments, a Type I SDF comes with greater risks, in terms of potential performance, and preconditions (i.e. local skills and expertise) that may not be readily obtainable.

Intersecting Politics

Although investment tasks can be outsourced to talented people around the world, and operations can be simplified to minimize complexity, a fund's relationship with politicians will always be a challenge. Indeed, complete separation of the sovereign fund from the sovereign sponsor is highly unlikely. There is an inherent link between the fund and the sponsor, and this is generally reflected in the mandate of the fund and its long-term performance. Autonomy is relative, not absolute. In effect, the long-term health of the fund and therefore the outcomes of its investment strategy are at risk if the sovereign sponsor is inherently unstable and subject to periodic crises of legitimacy. What forms of government may be more conducive to one type of SDF over another?

For countries where governance is concentrated, such as an absolute monarchy for example, popular legitimacy does not present much of a challenge, at least most of the time. That is not to say that legitimacy does not matter. Rather, popular interests are represented differently and indirectly. As a result, a Type I SDF is more likely to have a certain freedom of action, such as in the implementation of an unencumbered long-term investment strategy, compared with a democratic political environment where calls for accountability come at regular intervals. Such prevailing conditions may be conducive to the establishment of a Type I SDF, but it raises the spectre that the fund may not have broader development goals. Indeed, the ruling authority may find it useful to establish a Type I SDF, but only as a means of maintaining its power, even if it helps ignite economic growth and development that seemingly benefits the population.

In countries where governance is distributed, as in democracies, popular legitimacy matters much more. Popular interests are directly represented and must be accounted for. Consequently, a Type I SDF may face particular problems. How does it resist political incursions to invest in certain projects or companies? How does it defend against arguments that its investments are not driven by politics? This does not mean that a Type I fund cannot function in such an environment. Nonetheless, these are very real questions. If they cannot be resolved through a governance architecture that is appropriate and robust from one period to the next it may be easier to establish a Type II fund in countries with distributed political authority.

Delegated authority is the model for many public pension funds in the developed world. Modern portfolio theory, which underlies the conventional global portfolio model, neutralizes politics. Delegation to third-party asset managers likewise neutralizes politics. Assuming the prospect of a cash dividend engenders demands for accountability and transparency that limits corruption and the misallocation of funds to special interests. The cash dividend buys public support. However, with greater popular legitimacy, demands for short-term performance may come at the expense of a long-term approach to investing.

Principles, Policies and Pitfalls

Any set of principles and policies must be adaptive because financial markets never stand still—all markets, whether public or private, developed or underdeveloped, evolve such that institutions can become prisoners of the past.[22] Financial crises come and go, some regional and some global in nature. In extreme circumstances, SDFs may be called upon to bail out their sponsors. How and why this might take place should be subject to discussion when the institution is established.

Building on our research and not withstanding some of the more fundamental policy choices and viability of a Type 1 SDF in different contexts, this section sets out principles and policies to guide the establishment and management of high-performance, strategic investment organizations. In doing so, we are mindful that these funds inevitably reflect their countries of origin, their intended purposes, and the distinctive attributes of countries and regions in the modern economy. Inevitably, our principles and policies are not specific. That being said, they provide a blueprint for the issues that governments must address in the establishment, governance and management of a SDF. We propose six principles and six policies below.

---

[22] Andrew W. Lo, *The adaptive markets hypothesis*, 30 THE JOURNAL OF PORTFOLIO MANAGEMENT (2004).

Principles of Governance

To prosper in global markets, SDFs must have a robust governance frame-work that can meet the expectations of foreign due diligence. Indeed, if a fund is to originate deals locally and bring in co-investors, it has to be able to prove it is accountable and reliable. To develop the trust of others, SDFs need to adopt universally accepted procedures, such as reporting and accounting, and provide this information to an independent board and the co-investment community. As such, the sponsor should consider the following principles, which offer a mechanism to characterize the rationale and stated purpose of the institution.

- *Measurement*: SDFs should have a summary, or headline, rate of return target. This will impart a risk tolerance to the management team as well as provide stakeholders an expected long-term performance benchmark by which to hold managers accountable. While the time horizon for this target may be long term, it should ensure discipline in the short and medium term by promising future measurement of stated commitments against results.
- *Coherence*: recognizing that the rate of return target typically stands for a set of development objectives, these objectives should not conflict, and, where possible, these objectives should be ordered in terms of their priority.
- *Supervision*: the sponsor should seek to imbue the SDF with world-class governance. In general, effective boards of directors are relatively small (seven to nine members), and combine representatives from the sponsor and the executive directors of the institution with a group of independent directors whose expertise and relevance is unquestioned.
- *Delegation*: SDFs operate in complex, local environments that demand independence of operation and investment in the context of a defined set of objectives. As such, there should be a separation of powers between the board and management team, which necessarily must come with formally delegated powers to the senior executives for framing and implementation of investment.
- *Accountability*: boards should be accountable to their government sponsor in accordance with the SDF's mandate, just as senior executives should be accountable to their boards of directors. With accountability comes transparency, and with transparency comes legitimacy.
- *Commerciality*: the purpose of setting up an investment vehicle separate from government agencies, such as central banks or ministries of finance, is

to create a credible third-party investor. The idea is to bring market discipline to sectors that may have never had it. The new vehicle should thus have a well-defined, commercial orientation that can guide management and decision-making, as well as help other investors understand and appreciate its mission.

Policies of Management

Having established the principles and rules governing the organization of the institution, and being mindful of the need for flexibility and the possibility of encountering extreme situations, we now turn to the policies of management. This refers to how an institution realizes its goals and objectives in the context of the above principles.

- *Marketability*: one test of an investment strategy is whether other market participants might view it as attractive enough to join an SDF in specific projects and/or certain investment opportunities. SDFs should thus position themselves as partners for and with other investors, even using the decisions of private investors (most likely foreign) as a catalyst to unlock the SDF's capital as projects evolve. SDFs are best when they do not replace private agents but complement private agents' goals and objectives.
- *Positioning*: SDFs will inevitably be asked to incubate opportunities that sometimes have outputs that are hard to define. As such, the test is whether the SDF can retain some control over the opportunity it was responsible for developing. Most importantly, is the SDF able to participate in the value that it created?
- *Capabilities*: an SDF must match its capabilities and resources (and those of its partners) to the nature and scope of its investment strategy. Excessive ambition introduces risks that are neither easily identified nor controlled. SDF performance is predicated on unrivalled expertise and knowledge of domestic and regional markets. SDFs must be able to source, assess, structure and de-risk (as appropriate) investment opportunities in a credible way that provides confidence to service providers or co-investment partners, such that the likelihood of a return objective will be met or exceeded. The best SDFs thus need investment teams of the highest possible quality with unambiguous records of excellence.
- *Phasing*: SDFs operate, almost by definition, in immature and private markets. As such, they inevitably incur far greater illiquidity than other beneficial investment organizations. The lack of liquidity demands a rigorous

process for monitoring and assessing performance at each phase of invest-ment because interim checkpoints are crucial for unlocking follow-on investment. Deliberately managing the investment process over phases also provides opportunities for dividing up and distributing risk to third parties.

- *Risk*: SDFs face idiosyncratic, project-specific risks rather than market risks. Recognizing the nature and scope of risks in any SDF investment process will inevitably need to go far beyond traditional risk models, including scenario planning, agent-based models and other qualitative factors.

- *Translation*: In instances where foreign investors and local government pri-orities conflict, SDFs can serve as points of contact between international investors and local policymakers so as to lock-in deals or deal with trickier transactions. SDFs, unlike foreign investors, are in a better position to lobby local governments on behalf of international communities through their links with their sponsors (in other words, their national government).

In summary, whereas SWFs rely upon public and private markets for the deploy-ment of their assets, SDFs rely upon the integrity of their management systems to realize long-term goals. Building this integrity and ensuring legitimacy can be difficult and expensive. But so too are white elephants, castles in the sky, and other kinds of show-pieces that reflect more upon the failure to establish bind-ing principles and policies than the shortcomings in SDFs as an organizational form. At the same time, perfection comes at a price. This may be reflected in a lack of flexibility, a slavish adherence to past practices, and a degree of account-ability that paralyzes innovation rather than rewarding innovation.

Pitfalls to Avoid

Although there is a lack of comprehensive data and information regarding the poor performance of certain SDFs, and not all failures can be accounted, we have identified three issues that SDFs and their sponsors should consider so as to avoid operational failure:

- *Deadweight loss*: SDFs should avoid investing in assets or conducting trans-actions that either the government or the free market could and may do on their own. If SDFs are intended to be catalytic in and through their opera-tions, there is no developmental value, social or otherwise, in encouraging investments that would have happened anyway.

- *Unintended consequences*: SDFs should learn from government and market failures so as to avoid making short-term decisions that lead to long-term problems at the domestic level. Consequently, funds should invest in their internal capabilities and resources in ways that create well-equipped research teams.
- *Bridges to nowhere*: development-oriented investment strategies require more (not less) rigour in identifying risks and undertaking investments than traditional strategies. At the very least, SDFs should be mindful of their organizational strengths and weaknesses so as to limit their operational scope and concentrate on their advantages.

Our hope is that these principles, policies and pitfalls provide would-be SDF sponsors a framework for their governance and management. Readers should note that these are points of reference, rather than recipes or fail-safe mechanisms for institutional performance.

Conclusions

Throughout this chapter we have tried to highlight the benefits that an SDF may bring, but without being naive about the prevailing political and institutional conditions that continue to exacerbate economic and social development in many developing countries. A crucial point of our argument is that there are no global solutions or global SDF designs that apply to all contexts. What works for one country may not be appropriate for another. It would be questionable for a capital-starved developing country in sub-Saharan Africa to copy a model followed by a high-income city-state or resource-wealthy social democracy in Europe. The design of any SDF must reflect the prevailing local conditions and resources. These conditions and resources include the political and institutional environment, the availability of human resources and expertise to execute an investment mandate or delegate a mandate to a domestic or foreign third-party manager, and what developmental needs are most pressing and likely to be of most benefit (e.g. investing in distributive justice against productive efficiency).

The sophistication of the fund and its operations should be reflected in the general sophistication of the immediate institutional environment. Said slightly differently, achieving sophistication in asset management takes considerable time and resources. Many SDFs from developing countries may find it difficult and costly to buy in expertise from abroad, let alone find the sufficient expertise at home necessary to operate a sophisticated and diverse investment strategy, particularly strategies related to strategic investment (i.e. a Type I SDF). This does not mean that it is impossible or typical of all developing countries, particularly as many have members of their diasporas that have honed their financial expertise in the capitals of global finance. Just consider the pool of global talent in London.

For many sponsors, particularly in low-income developing countries, a simple investment strategy aimed at achieving at least market returns in a global portfolio is arguably the most prudent choice in the first instance. In many contexts it may also be the most politically feasible strategy, or at least the strategy that is most popularly inclusive. However, the design process of an SDF cannot be thought of as a task completed in a short period of time. While the mission should not stray too far from its original position, the fund and its investment strategy can become more sophisticated over time. This may, for example, allow a Type II SDF to expand its remit, establishing other funds with more sophisticated remits (e.g. a Type I SDF focused on local private equity).

What is important to stress, in sum, is that establishing a sovereign fund and sustaining its capacity over the long term confronts the same problems already constraining economic growth and development. The prevailing institutional and political reality cannot be easily ignored. For example, political elites and interest groups may simply use the fund for their own gain and patronage activities. Ultimately, sovereign funds of any sort are not a panacea for the challenges that constrain economic development and long-term prosperity. A sovereign fund may help overcome history and geography, but it is still subject to the prevailing institutional and political environment. If the sovereign fund is not part of a wider effort, its chances of success and likely benefits over the long term may be doubtful.

9

Ten Pillars for Centennial Outperformance

Financial markets have been the beneficiaries of a three-decade decline in interest rates. This has meant that generous passive market returns have added to overall portfolio returns. Adding value above market returns in this period was nice, but it was not critical for most funds to achieve their objectives. Looking to the future, however, we see a far more modest outlook for market returns, heightening the importance of adding value above benchmarks. Indeed, value-added returns will become a significant contributor to overall portfolio returns in the future. We believe that delivering this value requires a high quality, performance-driven organization. It is for this reason we think it is imperative for beneficiary institutions to reconsider, revise and, where necessary, restructure the way they approach investing.

Many investors regard themselves as being in one of the most challenging investment environment for decades. They are all asking the question: How can we generate returns needed to meet long-term policy benchmarks and mandates? In answering this question, we start with some principles, noting that the job of an institutional investor is to take money and turn it into more money. That's really all that investors do. Put another way, the product that institutional investors all make is universal: they produce returns. And to deliver returns, investors, for the most part, use the same set of inputs. To their initial stock of financial capital, they add human capital, informational advantages and processes. If these four inputs (capital, people, information and process) are combined effectively, an investment organization is more likely to achieve its objectives and deliver the necessary returns. While this may sound simple, the production of investment returns is complicated by

© The Editor(s) (if applicable) and The Author(s) 2016
J. Singh Bachher et al., *The New Frontier Investors*,
DOI 10.1057/978-1-137-50857-7_9

the fact that most investors' inputs vary a great deal in terms of their quality, quantity and source. And this variation has led to the emergence of many standards or 'models' of institutional investment that seek to combine inputs in different ways, such as the US endowment model, the Canadian pension fund model, or the Norwegian sovereign fund model. In each of these models, the quality, quantity and source of inputs drives investors in very different organizational directions.

Given the importance of the inputs in all these models, we have focused in this book on the ways in which different investors can foster, develop and use their own inputs. We've tried to develop input-oriented 'blueprints' of organizational design, institutional governance and investment management. We've stressed the importance of innovation; the importance of human capital but also its variety; the possibilities of insourcing; the promise of platforms for collaboration and co-investment; the potential for expanding the global footprint of investment organizations; the nuances of transparency; as well as the design of beneficiary institutions for development, reminding our community that finance is ultimately about facilitating the growth and development of the real economy. In all of these cases, we've sought to equip institutional investors with tools for organizing and equipping investment funds with the best inputs for the different contexts and strategies, while recognizing that there is no 'one-size-fits-all' strategy.

At the University of California's Office of the Chief Investment Officer (UCOCIO), we see the themes of this book critical to the development of our own organization. Hence, we are putting our words into action. As such, this case study provides a fitting conclusion to the narrative we've developed over the previous eight chapters. We recognize that it can be difficult to apply any of the blueprints discussed in this book directly to the UCOCIO. In our perspective, becoming an effective investor demands as much self-knowledge as it does knowledge about the models of finance or economics. Investors have to blend their own inputs in unique ways. And yet, we also believe that the theory, logic and methodology that drove the body of research that sustains the arguments of this book could serve us well in forming our own strategic plans. And we hope it provides inspiration to others.

With thoughtful consideration of all the material that has gone into this book and the research that informs it, we have begun to evaluate our own organization, specifically assessing how we should manage the four main products we run (i.e., working capital, defined benefit pension, defined contribution pension, and endowment). We believe there is a great opportunity to combine our unique and proprietary inputs with the pillars of investment success that we've outlined in this book to achieve our long-term objectives. The objective of this exercise is not to try to describe how all endowments should run their business—though our pillars may be relevant to others—we are simply trying to reflect on what pillars should guide the UCOCIO's thinking as a thoughtful and high-performance long-term investor. For our readers in the investment community, it is about showing how one organization is taking seriously the challenges of investing that will shape the investment environment for decades to come.

The UCOCIO has been managing money for 80 years, and we expect, as an office, to be managing money 80 years from now. The primary goal of the endowment is to provide income to the University of California, while at least maintaining the real value of the endowment capital. To date, this goal has been translated into a rate of return target of at least 4.75 per cent a year over any rolling four-year period. Generally speaking, however, we simply see ourselves as being charged with supporting the mission and operations of a university that plans to exist in perpetuity. This perspective puts our office in the position of being a very long-term investor. We do not have to respond to every bump in the road in a quest for month-by-month returns. Instead, we can brace ourselves for the 'radical uncertainty' that inevitably comes with capitalism and its associated forces of creative destruction. In fact, we can position ourselves to take advantage of the volatility in markets by adopting a long-run posture and having a sense for long-run value. We think of this as investing centenially—investing for the next 100 years.

In this chapter we outline the set of principles and policies (what we call 'pillars') that guide the design of the University of California endowment. When Jagdeep Bachher took up the position of Chief Investment Officer of the Regents in 2014, the first thing we did was set the beliefs for the organization. Starting in January 2015, we then dedicated four months to answering the question, as a management team, as to how our endowment would fulfill its mandate. In what follows, we outline the 10 pillars of success that emerged from the working groups, our review of the literature and a series of case studies of like-minded peers. These pillars, in conjunction with our investment beliefs, should serve to guide this office for decades to come. With this in mind, please note that this text does not intend to deliver a detailed set of prescriptions to the present and future managers of the UCOCIO. Rather, it assumes and anticipates that the investment organization and its managers will interpret these pillars in the context of the specific needs and constraints of the UCOCIO at a time and place in the future—that the projects accompanying each pillar will change over time. We also recognize that the pillars are aspirational and often ambitious, especially when taken as a whole. This means that implementing each pillar may require years of staging. Even so, the pillars represent our attempt to present a concise and simple set of points for attention and action in our investment organization in the decade ahead.

The Pillars of Our Future Success

In this section, we offer our 10 pillars of success, which represent the principles for how we believe the UCOCIO should operate in the decades ahead. Please note that each pillar is equally important to the other, albeit listed sequentially to convey a sense that one may be required before the other can be implemented effectively.

Pillar 1: Less Is More

Many institutional investors around the world—our peers—are focused on how they can grow. The prospect of working with an increasingly misaligned set of intermediaries in global financial centres has driven many pension, endowment and sovereign funds to search for new ways to access markets and assets directly. Many have decided to increase their head count, improve internal systems and controls, and even expand their global footprint by setting up overseas offices—all in the name of reducing reliance on the for-profit financial industry. We accept that this approach offers a more aligned access point to financial markets than other investment models, including the 'endowment model', but we also think the pendulum may have swung too far.

At the UCOCIO, we think a new generation of institutional investors will take a different and smaller approach based on tight, excellent teams managing a concentrated portfolio of high quality assets. We also believe that technology will empower these excellent individuals by streamlining processes and rapidly converting data and information into actionable knowledge. Empowered by world-class technology, we expect the next generation of investors—among which we hope to count ourselves—to creatively combine people, process and information in new ways. At the UCOCIO, we are thus focused on how we can excel in a small set of well-defined areas.

In practice, we are working to reduce the number of decisions we have to make, the number of relationships we have to manage, the number of items in our portfolio, the number of external managers we use, and so on. We have to question whether it is wise that our actively managed public equity book currently has 12,000 stocks. We also question if an endowment of $10 billion should have 200 private equity line items that range between $1 million and $5 million. We tend to think we'd be better off providing a world-class team with a laser focus in areas where we can outperform the market. And where we can't do that, we will work hard to identify low cost external service providers for market exposures.

To execute on this pillar, we will need to implement a few key projects in the next few years:

- Heuristics: we may want to establish quantitative targets for the key areas in which organizations can creep up in size, such as 'line items in a portfolio' (250) or external managers (100).
- Excellence: we will need to develop a culture of accountability in which individuals accept and embrace the risks that come with a 'less is more' culture.

Pillar 2: Risk Rules Everything

The risk tools available in the marketplace are extremely helpful in unpacking and understanding complex institutional investment portfolios. But they are incomplete. The 'value at risk' and standard deviation measures, which are sometimes supplemented by scenario planning and stress tests, fail to help us understand how crises propagate through markets. As such, existing tools will not guide us through the next great market crash and the ensuing market contagion moving into secondary and tertiary markets. We thus believe new risk models that, for example, use crowd-sourcing to help predict how a liquidity event will move through tangential markets, are needed.

Within the UCOCIO, we are working to identify, assess, manage and monitor a plethora of risks. From operations through to the investment team, we want everybody to be risk managers. In this regard, we are working to embed the language and actions of risk management into everything we do. By allocating assets according to the risk elements that drive returns, we expect to create more diversity compared with our benchmarks and generate more return per unit of risk.

To do this effectively, however, we will need new processes to formalize and standardize organizational expectations around risk as well as to come to some agreement as to the exact risks that should be measured across all assets and opportunities and used in investment decisions. Inevitably, investments will have some risks that are quantifiable and can be communicated in monetary terms (market and active risk), while other risks will be less easy to communicate because of their subjective and long-term nature. In both cases, a standardized approach for approvals will help to make sure that we are capturing all the important risks when we make an investment decision.

To execute this pillar, we will need to implement several projects:

- Risk tools: to bolster our understanding of risk, we need to work creatively with data and analytics providers to develop new, forward-looking risk tools.
- Standards: a set of standard risks should be developed, maintained and demanded from all of our research, due diligence and approvals process. This will lead to a common risk language.
- Risk allocation: the team responsible for developing asset allocation strategy should also be responsible for ensuring that the necessary risk factors are being considered—across the entire portfolio and within specific assets—and that our portfolio is risk *and* asset allocated.
- Capabilities: because we invest in managers, which is what we do 90 per cent of the time in private and public markets (stocks), we need to manage risks through an overlay based on our views. This may require us to develop an internal capability to run a risk overlay to manage our risks efficiently.
- Culture: we need a cultural shift to allow the UCOCIO to operate as a single team; one that can assess a single portfolio, while respecting the changing nature of each of our product lines' risks. We need to work as a team to assess our decisions and then own the decisions as a team.
- Organization: to ensure all of the above projects are realized, we may need a thoughtfully designed, management investment committee (MIC) that can serve as a manifestation of our risk framework and culture. In addition, we may need to combine the existing 'group CIO' with a series of 'product CIOs'. The latter would have responsibility for managing the risks of each underlying product.

Pillar 3: Concentration

After risk management, portfolio construction is the primary tool to help the UCOCIO achieve its goals. In theory, portfolio construction takes a fund's unique characteristics, objectives, investment beliefs, risk tolerance, strategic ambitions and constraints to help develop a rigorous investment process that includes risk measurement, risk taking, risk monitoring and risk reporting. The over-arching idea of portfolio construction is to maximize the amount of return we generate per unit of risk and per dollar of cost at the level of the total portfolio.

In line with the pillars above, at the UCOCIO we prefer to construct a portfolio made up of a concentrated set of assets that we understand deeply (as opposed to holding many assets we barely understand). We will thus look to diversify our assets as much as is required but no more. By reducing the number of investments in our portfolio, we believe we can reduce unwanted risks and increase wanted returns. New research shows that the cost of diversification may in fact outweigh its benefits, especially in asset classes such as hedge funds and private equity.[1]

The UCOCIO will thus be guided by a simple philosophy of portfolio construction: every asset added to the portfolio must significantly contribute to both alpha and diversification at the total portfolio level. To construct portfolios like this, we will need to have a single team that is capable of assessing deals across the portfolio. We are not averse to complexity, but we want to ensure we fully appreciate the component risks of every investment we make and then diversify those risks at the total portfolio level. Moreover, we want to add value to our partners and investments in any way we can. Can we realistically sit on 100 advisory boards (as we currently do) and hope to add any value at all to any of them? We think we may need to concentrate.

To execute this pillar, we will need to address the following:

- Mapping: portfolio construction revolves around mapping our investment objectives to the appropriate asset classes and also mapping asset classes for their own risk and return characteristics (e.g., inflation sensitivity, directionality, growth and rates).
- Data: we need to be able to determine three numbers for every opportunity: expected return, overall risk and correlation. To do this we will require new systems that can house the wealth of data and provide 'on the fly' reporting.
- Themes: we may need a 'theme team' that will develop the ideas underpinning our portfolio. This team will first define what constitutes a top idea or theme and then determine how to revise themes and, importantly, how to implement them. This team should be agnostic to the access point.
- Standards: investment proposals will need to be standardized and systematized, balancing the need to move fast and be proactive with the diligence requirements of the organization. We may also need a reference portfolio for each of our products to assess performance at the portfolio level.

---

[1] William W. Jennings & Brian C. Payne, *Fees Eat Diversification's Lunch*, available at SSRN 2543031 (2014).

Pillar 4: Creativity Pays Dividends

Institutional investment organizations are not often thought of as being innovative organizations. At the UCOCIO, we reject this view and choose to focus on developing competitive portfolios, even if that can at times mean unconventional or uncomfortable thinking and doing. We adopt this view because of our belief that financial markets are constantly changing ecosystems. Good ideas are ephemeral, and, importantly, there are rewards for spotting opportunities early and acting in an entrepreneurial manner. We also believe that new approaches offer, almost by definition, a less competitive access point for attractive assets, which means a creative investor can reduce fees and costs associated with investment execution.

We believe that being a successful investor requires a persistent focus on "what's new" and "what's possible". As such, we plan to build a dedicated innovation function within our organization, which is rare in the world of institutional investment. This group will have accountability for launching unique vehicles that leverage the Office of the CIO's competitive advantages (e.g., UC Ventures). The group will also have accountability for launching the CIO's special projects, as well as developing deep relationships with peers and aligned partners that may offer inspiration and opportunity. For example, over the past year we've forged deep relationships with a handful of dynamic and thoughtful family offices. In the future, we will continue to seek out collaborative, long-term investment organizations (of any stripe) as partners if they have a capacity to be innovative and aligned.

Executing this pillar, will require us to consider:

- Organization: we may need to create a team of entrepreneurial individuals within the UCOCIO that can incubate, validate and develop innovative ideas before handing them off to the core portfolio teams.
- Independence: while all new projects and platforms will have to fit into the themes being developed by the above-mentioned theme team, the innovation team may also need to have some capital earmarked for their own special projects. This will allow a longer period of incubation before bringing projects to the investment committee for a formal thumbs up or down assessment.
- Technology: we may need new tools and technologies to map our networks and characteristics so as to identify R&D projects as well as support the projects we are launching.

Pillar 5: Putting Information into Action

Knowledge is about forming beliefs and making commitments; it is about putting information and data into action. As this implies, knowledge goes to the heart of investment decision-making. To develop superior knowledge, an investment organization must appreciate the data and information required to create knowledge. It must then mobilize the resources to maintain that knowledge. And, finally, it has to be able to apply the knowledge to exploit knowledge. In sum, superior knowledge, which drives superior returns, is truly a function of an investment organization's design, character and culture.

The view that superior knowledge drives superior returns, a seemingly obvious observation to many active managers, actually contradicts some of the dominant frameworks used by investors.[2] The Efficient Market Hypothesis and the Capital Asset Pricing Model, for example, claim that capital markets are efficient and that no asset manager has superior knowledge over the broader market, even suggesting that all possible information is reflected in current market prices and excess returns are simply a function of the level of risk taken. While these theories may explain why many investors do little in the domain of knowledge management, it seems to us a mistaken and erroneous assumption upon which to build an investment portfolio.

As such, at the UCOCIO we believe that a proactive approach to the creation, maintenance and exploitation of knowledge will be critical to our success. We are thus developing strategies to manage and mobilize superior knowledge in the context of our investing. We consider ourselves remarkably lucky to be sitting at the heart of such a knowledge-rich environment: the University of California. But to take advantage of the university and other sources of knowledge, we must have the right systems, policies and processes in place.

For this pillar, we will to act on the following:

- Collaboration: we must develop our culture of collaboration, encouraging internal teams to be proactive about sharing important information across the organization. This may require incentives to encourage knowledge management. It may also require breaking down silos.
- Data: we need to invest in high quality data infrastructure and then use our data to populate powerful systems to track portfolios, risks and networks.

---

[2] Eduard Van Gelderen & Ashby H. B. Monk, *Knowledge Management in Asset Management*, Available at SSRN 2642467 (2015).

- Knowledge management: we need to invest in a system that can institutionalize our knowledge by triggering meeting reports, network updates and the sharing of research outputs, among other things, more routinely.

Pillar 6: A Committed Team

Human capital is one of the key inputs required to produce investment returns. It's for this reason that financial services professionals command such high salaries; those that have a track record of performance are particularly sought after. At the UCOCIO, we must attract high calibre investors and leaders to be successful. This includes talented professionals but also team players who can adopt our long-term culture and objectives. As a public agency investor, many would see us as inherently limited in the kinds of people we can recruit. Going forward, however, we are working to implement policies that are aligned with the expectations of the industry as well as use the university's brand and its location to attract top investment managers and leaders. Moreover, we will focus our recruiting where we are likely to be the most successful; what we call the grey, the green and the grounded:

- Grey: public pensions and endowments are competitive in hiring experienced individuals. Generally, such individuals have had successful careers in the private sector over 15–25 years. They've made their money and are now interested in giving back or, depending on the circumstances, escaping the rat race. At the UCOCIO, we offer these people a mission-oriented organization where they can practise their trade through to the end of their careers and serve as mentors to younger employees.
- Green: public pension and endowments are generally competitive in attracting early career individuals. At this stage, having up to five years' experience, the disparity between public and private sector salaries is at its lowest. Moreover, we believe we can offer a young recruit 20 years of experience and relationships for five years of hard work. There are many individuals that will give up some current income to accelerate their career prospects and opportunities.
- Grounded: public pensions and endowments are also competitive at hiring people who are tied to the sponsoring institution or region because of history, family, identity or affinity. In our case, we have been remarkably successful in attracting some of the 1.6 million talented UC alumni and also people who want to live in California.

In summary, we will develop a small, coherent team of the best people we can find. We've been quite successful in using the green, grey and grounded attributes to bring world-class people on board. To achieve our aim, we need to work on:

- Talent mix: we need to do an inventory and revise the mix of direct investment, risk allocation and manager selection people we have and need in the organization. We think a healthy mix would be to have an equal balance of these three characteristics.
- Careers: we will formalize a career path for junior and mid-career staff.
- Pools: we will develop centralized teams of pooled resources that will be drawn on to staff up 'opportunity swat teams'.
- Pay: we will review our practices to ensure they are aligned with industry expectations.

Pillar 7: The UC Advantage

The best investments tend to be found in areas where markets are inefficient and where information does not freely travel. It may be an oversimplification, but if an opportunity fits in a box or a silo, it iss probably overbid and over-valued. The best investors use their unique characteristics in a deliberate attempt to move into markets with minimal competition. To do this, however, investment organizations must understand and leverage their *unique* characteristics. Put another way, maximizing the returns that can be achieved per unit of risk and per fee dollar spent often asks an organization to think hard about its own advantages and be proactive in using those advantages in the context of broader market forces.

At the UCOCIO, we have a variety of characteristics that, if cultivated appropriately, should be a source of persistent, high quality investment opportunities. We are a large, long-term, public, Californian investment organization sitting at the heart of Silicon Valley.

The University of California is one of the premier public research institutions in the world. It is comprised of 10 campuses, five medical centres, and three national laboratories. With 233,000 students, 190,000 faculty and staff, and 1.7 million living alumni, new ideas and groundbreaking technologies are commonplace and often underpin the creation of successful companies. But the scale and scope of the ecosystem is often underappreciated. Consider the following:

- 8–10 per cent of the total academic research funds provided by the US government go to UC.
- Over the financial year 2013–2014, UC spent $5.7 billion on funded research projects.
- During 2013–2014, university researchers submitted 1727 inventions.
- 324 companies have emerged directly from the university's technology transfer office in the past five years.
- Since 2005, UC startups have attracted $5 billion in venture capital.

This is an innovation ecosystem that is unparalleled on a global scale, and we sit at the centre of it. We believe we can leverage the unique characteristics of the UC ecosystem in ways that drive investment returns. As such, we are working in a highly transparent manner to engage and capitalize on our unique set of relationships.

For this pillar, our projects include:

- Team: we may need a dedicated relationship team sourcing opportunities, broadly defined, from within the UC ecosystem. This team would also be responsible for helping portfolio companies and managers connect with UC resources.
- Sourcing: we need to define the people in the organization who will be responsible for discovering investment opportunities within our themes and from our privileged access points (including Silicon Valley, UC and our peers).
- Collaboration: we should reinforce collaboration—internally among individuals and externally among partners and peers—as a cornerstone of our sourcing advantage.
- Capabilities: when opportunities arise from our peers and managers, we need have the organizational flexibility to quickly evaluate and take advantage of these opportunities.

Pillar 8: Execution and Alignment

The financial innovations of the past decades have substantially increased the complexity of the instruments and services offered by the financial services industry. With all this complexity, however, have come new and under-appreciated costs, as the increasing sophistication has resulted in concomitant opacity. Take, as an example, the fact that in 1950 the financial services industry enjoyed a 10 per cent share of US corporate profits. Today, that number is 40 per cent. In short, the job of pension and endowment management is far more difficult today than it was in the past, as the fees and costs of financial intermediation have become more difficult to identify, rationalize and minimize.

As a long-term investor reliant on third party intermediaries for execution, we find this problematic. In our view, fees and costs are nothing more than incentives for our managers, which means that for us to fully understand the incentives we are creating in our managers we *have* to understand the fees and costs. And if a third party manager is not willing to provide a detailed—borderline forensic—breakdown of how it actually makes its money from managing our money, then we should walk away and pull our capital.

We are thus working to increase the transparency of all the products and services we consume. We are doing this because we want a better understanding of our investment risks (e.g., counterparty risk and inefficient structures,) as well as to reduce misalignment of interests—not to mention capture the risk-free returns that come from reducing the expenses on a portfolio without changing anything else about it.

In sum, we plan to pay considerable attention to fees and costs in the decade to come, as we believe that paying high fees to intermediaries today is a recipe for paying even higher fees to unaligned intermediaries tomorrow. Focusing on this pillar requires:

• Transparency: we must continue to try to understand the cost of external service providers.
• Systems: we must continue to develop capabilities focused on fees and costs.
• Alignment: the internal team needs to have a cultural change such that fees and costs become as important as anything else in an investment agreement.

Pillar 9: Leveraging Technology

To a large extent, the complexity of finance has been a function of more sophisticated technologies. These technologies, until recently, have served to empower and reinforce the hegemony of intermediaries, such as hedge funds. However, sitting on our perch here in Silicon Valley, we can see technology evolving to the point where it may challenge (rather than reinforce) the power of certain intermediaries.

We believe technology can help institutional investors streamline and strengthen operations, manage and distribute knowledge, access unique (and heretofore expensive) markets, and level the playing field with the private financial services industry generally. Technological innovation may come with growing pains and challenges, but it is not something we can ignore.

In our view, technology may help investors overcome the limitations of existing governance models. It may provide a means of collaborating with peer organizations. It can help minimize errors and biases, all of which will increase efficiency. Investors may be better placed to both understand their portfolios and be able to manage them more effectively. As such, at the UCOCIO, we expect technology will change the nature of financial intermediation and investment. The more the service is a commodity, the more it will be affected.

As such, we will continue to seek out innovative startups in Silicon Valley to ensure we are a model investment organization when it comes to adopting the latest technology. We recognize and accept the challenges that come with new technologies. In fact, we may seek some form of compensation from startups for being early adopters or cornerstone clients, in the form of discounts or warrants.

This pillar requires implementing projects about:

- Data: again, we have to develop our systems to provide normalized and aggregated data.
- Formalize adoption processes: we have to develop criteria for determining what tools and technologies are worth our time in bringing on board and the process for doing so.
- Selecting partners: we need to determine how best to form partnerships with technology companies in the domain of asset management and institutional investment.

Pillar 10: Centennial Performance

Because of our long history and, we expect, long future, we think of ourselves as investing centenially—that is, for the next 100 years. This centennial orientation drives us to incorporate a broader set of risks into our decision making than those organizations with shorter time horizons. We try to assess our portfolio with a lens that is attuned to the long-term, fundamental challenges facing society.

We do this because we believe that long-term risks, which include climate change, human rights and corporate governance, inevitably influence investment performance over the long run. Indeed, sustainable businesses are often more rooted in communities and resilient to the inevitable future crises, which means investing in them makes good business sense over the long run. Accordingly, we are making plans to be active in all those organizations that seek to develop tools and metrics for long-term risk measurement. As an example, we participate in the Principles for Responsible Investment set out by the United Nations, which place a priority on the incorporation of environmental, social and governance issues in the investment selection process. To address this pillar, we will need to consider:

- Frameworks: we need to finalize the ways in which long-term risk factors (i.e., environmental, social and governance issues) are incorporated in our investment decisions. This should not be tick-box but an opportunity to consider future scenarios in which assets may be affected differently.
- Assessments: we need to determine how we will assess managers and assets and what we will do with those assessments once we have them.
- Validation: we need to keep refining our thinking and understanding of 'long-term investing' to position our portfolio for financial outperformance.

Final Thoughts

In the past few decades, generous passive market returns have boosted overall portfolio returns. Adding value above market in this period was nice, but it was not critical for funds to achieve their objectives. Looking to the future, however, we are facing a more modest outlook for financial market returns, heightening the importance of adding value above benchmarks. Delivering these value-added returns will require a reconsideration of the way we assess, access and manage investment opportunities in the context of people, processes and information.

We are thus rethinking our approach to investing and how we collaborate internally and externally. We are becoming more focused on the efficiency of our processes for making investment decisions, as well as on our culture, data, risk, execution, fees, costs, and how we monitor our investments. With one portfolio and a common risk language, the UCOCIO should be able to assess opportunities across asset classes. Empowered by world-class technology, we should also be able to use our inherent characteristics in a deliberate way to move into markets with minimal competition, leveraging the UC brand wherever possible.

It's worth repeating here that we do all this to serve the University of California. We are acutely aware that higher returns mean greater income and support for the university and its campuses. This is our focus—today and for the coming century.

Bibliography

Acemoglu, Daron, and James A. Robinson. 2012. *Why nations fail: The origins of power, prosperity and poverty*, 1st ed. New York: Crown Publishers.

Aker, Jenny C., and Isaac M. Mbiti. 2010. Mobile phones and economic development in Africa. *The Journal of Economic Perspectives* 24(3): 207–232.

Akerlof, George A., and Robert J. Shiller. 2009. *Animal spirits: How human psychology drives the economy, and why it matters for global capitalism*. Princeton: Princeton University Press.

Ambachtsheer, Keith P. 2007. *Pension revolution: a solution to the pensions crisis*. Hoboken: Wiley.

Ambachtsheer, Keith P. 2011. How should pension funds pay their own people? *Rotman International Journal of Pension Management* 4(1): 18–25. doi:10.3138/rijpm.4.1.18.

Ang, Andrew, W. Goetzmann, and S. Schaefer. 2009. Evaluation of active management of the Norwegian Government Pension Fund—Global. https://www0.gsb.columbia.edu/faculty/aang/papers/report%20Norway.pdf. Accessed 26 March 2016.

Armendariz, Beatriz, and Jonathan Morduch. 2010. *The economics of microfinance*, 2nd ed. Cambridge, MA: MIT Press.

Auty, Richard M. 2001. *Resource abundance and economic development*. Oxford: Oxford University Press.

Bagnall, Sophie, and Edwin Truman. 2011. IFSWF report on compliance with the Santiago Principles: Admirable but flawed transparency. *Peterson Institute for International Economics Policy Brief*: 11–14.

Barbary, Victoria, Ashby Monk, and Touraya Triki. 2011. The new investment frontier: SWF investment in Africa. In *Braving the new world: Sovereign wealth fund investment in the uncertain times of 2010*, ed. V. Barbary and B. Bortolotti, 54–60. London: Monitor Group.

© The Editor(s) (if applicable) and The Author(s) 2016 **135**
J. Singh Bachher et al., *The New Frontier Investors*,
DOI 10.1057/978-1-137-50857-7

Bathelt, Harald, and Johannes Glückler. 2011. *The relational economy: Geographies of knowing and learning.* Oxford: Oxford University Press.

Baum, Joel A.C., and Brian S. Silverman. 2004. Picking winners or building them? Alliance, intellectual, and human capital as selection criteria in venture financing and performance of biotechnology startups. *Journal of Business Venturing* 19(3): 411–436.

Bertram, Robert, and Barbara Zvan. 2009. Pension funds and incentive compensation: A story based on the Ontario Teachers' experience. *Rotman International Journal of Pension Management* 2(1): 30–33. doi:10.3138/rijpm.2.1.30.

Bolton, Patrick, Frederic Samama, and Joseph Stiglitz (eds.). 2011. *Sovereign wealth funds and long-term investing.* New York: Columbia University Press.

Boschma, Ron. 2005. Proximity and innovation: A critical assessment. *Regional Studies* 39(1): 61–74. doi:10.1080/0034340052000320887.

Bygrave, William D., and Jeffry A. Timmons. 1992. *Venture capital at the crossroads.* Boston: Harvard Business Press.

Cahoy, Daniel R. 2012. Inverse enclosure: Abdicating the green technology landscape. *American Business Law Journal* 49(4): 805–857.

Chesbrough, Henry W. 2002. Making sense of corporate venture capital. *Harvard Business Review* 80(3): 90–99.

Christensen, Clayton. 2013. *The innovator's dilemma: When new technologies cause great firms to fail.* Boston: Harvard Business Review Press.

Clark, Gordon L. 2000. *Pension fund capitalism.* Oxford: Oxford University Press.

Clark, Gordon L. 2007. Expertise and representation in financial institutions: UK legislation on pension fund governance and US regulation of the mutual fund industry. *Twenty-First Century Society* 2(1): 1–23.

Clark, Gordon L. 2011. Fiduciary duty, statute, and pension fund governance: the search for a shared conception of sustainable investment. *Available at SSRN 1945257.*

Clark, Gordon L., and Ashby H.B. Monk. 2013. The scope of financial institutions: In-sourcing, outsourcing and off-shoring. *Journal of Economic Geography* 13(2): 279–298. doi:10.1093/jeg/lbs061.

Clark, Gordon L., and Roger C. Urwin. 2008. Best-practice pension fund governance. *Journal of Asset Management* 9(1): 2–21.

Clark, Gordon L., Adam D. Dixon, and Ashby H.B. Monk. 2013. *Sovereign wealth funds: Legitimacy, governance, and global power.* Princeton: Princeton University Press.

Collier, Paul, Rick Van Der Ploeg, Michael Spence, and Anthony J. Venables. 2010. Managing resource revenues in developing economies. *IMF Staff Papers* 57(1): 84–118.

Coval, Joshua D., and Tobias J. Moskowitz. 2001. The geography of investment: Informed trading and asset prices. *Journal of Political Economy* 109(4): 811–841.

Das, Udaibir S., Adnan Mazarei, Han van der Hoorn, and International Monetary Fund. 2010. *Economics of sovereign wealth funds: Issues for policymakers*. Washington, DC: International Monetary Fund.

Davis, Jeffrey M., Rolando Ossowski, and Annalisa Fedelino. 2003. *Fiscal policy formulation and implementation in oil-producing countries*. Washington, DC: International Monetary Fund.

Dixon, Adam D. 2008. The rise of pension fund capitalism in Europe: An unseen revolution? *New Political Economy* 13(3): 249–270.

Engelen, E., I. Ertürk, J. Froud, J. Sukhdev, A. Leaver, M. Moran, A. Nilsson, and K. Williams. 2011. *After the great complacence: Financial crisis and the politics of reform*. Oxford: Oxford University Press.

Florida, R., and M. Kenney. 1988. Venture capital, high technology and regional development. *Regional Studies* 22(1): 33–48. doi:10.1080/00343408812331344750.

Foster, Dean P., and H. Payton Young. 2010. Gaming performance fees by portfolio managers. *The Quarterly Journal of Economics* 125(4): 1435–1458.

Galer, Russell. 2002. Prudent person rule standard for the investment of pension fund assets. *OECD Financial Market Trends* 83: 43–75.

Gelpern, Anna. 2011. Sovereignty, accountability, and the wealth fund governance conundrum. *Asian Journal of International Law* 1(02): 289–320. doi:10.1017/S2044251310000391.

Geraats, Petra M. 2002. Central bank transparency. *The Economic Journal* 112(483): F532–F565.

Gertler, Meric S. 2003. Tacit knowledge and the economic geography of context, or the undefinable tacitness of being (there). *Journal of Economic Geography* 3(1): 75–99.

Gompers, Paul A., and Josh Lerner. 1999. What drives venture capital fundraising? *NBER working papers* (6906).

Griffith-Jones, Stephanie, and José A. Ocampo. 2011. The rationale for sovereign wealth funds: A developing country perspective. In *Sovereign wealth funds and long-term investing*, ed. P. Bolton, F. Samama, and J. Stiglitz. New York: Columbia University Press.

Gylfason, Tor. 2011. Natural resource endowment: A mixed blessing? *CESifo Working paper series* (3353).

Haberly, Daniel. 2011. Strategic sovereign wealth fund investment and the new alliance capitalism: A network mapping investigation. *Environment and Planning A* 43(8): 1833–1852.

Hargadon, Andrew B., and Martin Kenney. 2012. Misguided policy? Following venture capital into clean technology. *California Management Review* 54(2): 118.

IFSWF. 2011. IFSWF members' experiences in the application of the Santiago Principles: Report prepared by the IFSWF Sub-committee 1 and the Secretariat in collaboration with the Members of the IFSWF. International Forum of Sovereign Wealth Funds.

Jennings, William W., and Brian C. Payne. 2014. Fees eat diversification's lunch. *Available at SSRN 2543031.*

Kaplan, Steven N., and Antoinette Schoar. 2005. Private equity performance: Returns, persistence, and capital flows. *The Journal of Finance* 60(4): 1791–1823.

Koedijk, Kees, and Alfred Slager. 2011. *Investment beliefs: A positive approach to institutional investing.* Houndmills/Basingstoke/Hampshire/New York: Palgrave Macmillan.

Lai, Karen P.Y. 2012. Differentiated markets: Shanghai, Beijing and Hong Kong in China's financial centre network. *Urban Studies* 49(6): 1275–1296.

Lamfalussy, Alexandre. 2001. Towards an integrated European financial market. *World Economy* 24(10): 1287–1294.

Levitt, Raymond E., Wang, C.-M. A., Ho, P. S., and Amy Javernick-Will. 2011. A contingency theory of organizational strategies for facilitating knowledge sharing in engineering organizations. *Global Projects Center working papers* (64).

Lewis, Michael. 2003. *Moneyball: The art of winning an unfair game,* 1st ed. New York: W. W. Norton.

Lo, Andrew W. 2004. The adaptive markets hypothesis. *The Journal of Portfolio Management* 30(5): 15–29.

MacIntosh, Jody, and Tom Scheibelhut. 2012. How large pension funds organize themselves: Findings from a unique 19-fund survey. *Rotman International Journal of Pension Management* 5(1): 34–40. doi:10.3138/rijpm.5.1.34.

Maddison, Angus. 2001. *The world economy: A millennial perspective.* Paris: Development Centre of the Organisation for Economic Co-operation and Development.

Malloy, Christopher J. 2005. The geography of equity analysis. *The Journal of Finance* 60(2): 719–755. doi:10.1111/j.1540-6261.2005.00744.x.

Marcus, Alfred, Joel Malen, and Shmuel Ellis. 2013. The promise and pitfalls of venture capital as an asset class for clean energy investment research questions for organization and natural environment scholars. *Organization & Environment* 26(1): 31–60.

Markham, Jerry W. 2011. *A financial history of the United States,* vol. 2. Armonk: M.E. Sharpe.

Mathonet, Pierre-Yves, and Thomas Meyer. 2008. *J-curve exposure: Managing a portfolio of venture capital and private equity funds.* Chichester: Wiley.

Monk, Ashby H.B. 2009. Recasting the sovereign wealth fund debate: Trust, legitimacy, and governance. *New Political Economy* 14(4): 451–468.

Moss, Todd. 2011. Oil to cash: Fighting the resource curse through cash transfers. *Center for Global Development working papers* (237).

Mulcahy, Diane, Bill Weeks, and Harold S. Bradley. 2012. *We have met the enemy and he is us: Lessons from twenty years of the Kauffman foundation's investment in venture capital funds and the triumph of hope over experience.* Ewing Marion Kauffman Foundation.

Murphy, L., and P. Edwards. 2003. *Bridging the valley of death: Transitioning from public to private sector financing*. Golden: National Renewable Energy Laboratory.

Nanda, Ramana, Ken Younge, and Fleming Lee. 2014. Innovation and entrepreneurship in renewable energy. In *The changing frontier: Rethinking science and innovation policy*. Chicago: University of Chicago Press.

Norton, Joseph J. 2010. The Santiago Principles for sovereign wealth funds: A case study on international financial standard-setting processes. *Journal of International Economic Law* 13(3): 645–662. doi:10.1093/jiel/jgq034.

Patrick, Hugh. 1966. Financial development and economic growth in underdeveloped countries. *Economic Development and Cultural Change* 14(2): 174–189.

Pollard, Jane, and Michael Samers. 2013. Governing Islamic finance: Territory, agency, and the making of cosmopolitan financial geographies. *Annals of the Association of American Geographers* 103(3): 710–726. doi:10.1080/00045608.2011.628256.

Rappaport, Andrew. 2005. The economics of short-term performance obsession. *Financial Analysts Journal* 61(3): 65–79.

Robinson, Joan. 1952. *The rate of interest, and other essays*. London: Macmillan & Co.

Rose, Paul. 2009. Sovereign wealth fund investment in the shadow of regulation and politics. *Georgetown Journal of International Law* 40(4): 1207–1237.

Ross, Michael L. 2012. *The oil curse: How petroleum wealth shapes the development of nations*. Princeton: Princeton University Press.

Sahlman, William A. 1990. The structure and governance of venture-capital organizations. *Journal of Financial Economics* 27(2): 473–521.

Santiso, Javier. 2009. Sovereign development funds: Key actors in the shifting wealth of nations. *Revue d'Économie Financière* 9(1): 291–315.

Sass, Steven A. 1997. *The promise of private pensions: The first hundred years*. Cambridge, MA: Harvard University Press.

Schumpeter, Joseph. 1934. *The theory of economic development: An inquiry into profits, capital, credit, interest, and the business cycle, Harvard economic studies*. Cambridge, MA: Harvard University Press.

Storper, Michael, and Anthony J. Venables. 2004. Buzz: Face-to-face contact and the urban economy. *Journal of Economic Geography* 4(4): 351–370.

Teece, David J. 2000. *Managing intellectual capital: Organizational, strategic, and policy dimensions*. Oxford: Oxford University Press.

Truman, Edwin M. 2010. *Sovereign wealth funds: Threat or salvation?* Washington, DC: Peterson Institute for International Economics.

Turner, Adair. 2010. *What banks do, what should they do and what public policies are needed to ensure best result for the real economy?* London: Cass Business School.

van der Ploeg, Frederick, and Anthony J. Venables. 2012. Harnessing windfall revenues: Optimal policies for resource—Rich developing economies. *The Economic Journal* 121(551): 1–30. doi:10.1111/j.1468-0297.2010.02411.x.

van Gelderen, Eduard, and Ashby H. B. Monk. 2015. Knowledge management in asset management. *Available at SSRN 2642467*.

Vise, David A., and Mark Malseed. 2006. *The Google story—Inside the hottest business, media and technology success of our times*. London: Pan Macmillan.

Wiltbank, Robert, and Warren Boeker. Angel investor performance project: Data overview. http://sites.kauffman.org/pdf/angel_groups_111207.pdf. Accessed 26 March 2016.

Wójcik, Dariusz. 2011. *The global stock market: Issuers, investors, and intermediaries in an uneven world*. Oxford: Oxford University Press.

Yeung, Henry. 2011. From national development to economic diplomacy? Governing Singapore's sovereign wealth funds. *The Pacific Review* 24(5): 625–652.

Zider, Bob. 1998. How venture capital works. *Harvard Business Review* 76(6): 131–139.

Index

A

absolute transparency, 92
Abu Dhabi Investment Authority
    (ADIA), 6, 75
AIMCo. *See* Alberta Investment
    Management Corporation
    (AIMCo)
Alaska Permanent Fund, 6
Alberta Heritage Savings Trust Fund,
    3n2
Alberta Investment Management
    Corporation (AIMCo), 3n2, 12,
    29, 33–4, 74
alignment, with fund strategy, 62
alternative assets, 31
Anglo-American countries, 2
APG Group, 19–20
asset owners, 1, 2, 7, 8, 50, 51
Australia
    capital markets, 10
    centres of global finance, 10
    compulsory pension savings, 4
    economy, 10–11
    ratio of pension assets to GDP, 4
    superannuation industry, 10–11
Australian Future Fund, 3

B

Bachher, Jagdeep, 121
belief systems, 16–18, 20–3
beneficiary financial institutions,
    17–19, 25, 29, 35, 57
beneficiary investors, 24–5
better governance, 16–17, 19
Black Coral Capital, 42
booming markets, 16

C

Canada, 5, 12, 31
Canadian benchmarking company, 30
Canadian pension funds, 31, 33, 120
Capital Asset Pricing Model, 21
capital-intensive green investment, 71
capital-intensive industries, 69

Note: Page number followed by 'n' refers to footnotes.

© The Editor(s) (if applicable) and The Author(s) 2016
J. Singh Bachher et al., *The New Frontier Investors*,
DOI 10.1057/978-1-137-50857-7

capital, sources of, 72
CEM, 30–1
centennial performance, 133
centres of global finance, 11
CFIUS. *See* Committee on Foreign
    Investment in the United States
    (CFIUS)
Chile, pension savings in, 4
China
    economy, 11
    financial centre in, 11
China Investment Corporation, 6
choice of platform, 50–1
Clark, Gordon, 25, 39
Cleantech Syndicate, 42, 49
    implementation, 45–7
    investments, 44–5
    motivation, 42–3
    responsibilities, 44
    structure, 44
co-investment vehicles and platforms
    alliance, 48–9
    choice of platform, 50–1
    Cleantech Syndicate, 49
    seed, 50
collaboration
    benefits and challenges of, 40–2
    framework of, 50
collateral returns, 104
Colorado Public Employees Retirement
    Association, 4
Committee on Foreign Investment in
    the United States (CFIUS), 84
conventional finance wisdom, 34, 35,
    103
conventional organizations, 4
conversion of information, 54
core beliefs, 21, 22
crafting investment beliefs, 21
creative collaboration model, 79
creativity pays dividends, 126–7
Crown corporation, 33
culture, governance and, 61–2

D

deal flow, 41, 48, 53–5, 99
development fund, types of, 107–8
direct investment, 30–1
direct investor, 31
distributive justice, 106–7
diversification, 24, 41
DP World, 84
Dutch disease, 101, 107, 108
Dutch pension funds, 13, 19–20
Dutch public sector pension plan, 19

E

East Asian countries, SWFs, 101
economic jargon, 70
economies of scale, 20
Efficient Market Hypothesis and the
    Capital Asset Pricing Model,
    127
emerging markets, 31
Employee Retirement Income Security
    Act of 1974 (ERISA), 85
EU Directive on Institutions for
    Occupational Retirement
    Provision (2003), 85
European market, 12

F

face-to-face contact, 53, 57
falsifiability, 22
federal regulations, 85
finance, geography of, 7–10
    centres of global finance, 11
    large frontier cities, 10–11
    small cities on distant frontier,
        11–12
    small cities on frontier, 12–13
finance, two views of, 110–11
financial centres, 53
financial innovations, 131
financial institutions, 101

financial investors, identity groups of, 72

financial markets, 18, 119

financial system, 1, 12

foreign-denominated assets, 101

foreign investors, 54, 102

framing transparency, 92

frontier investors, 17, 29, 54, 97

fund strategy, alignment with, 62

G

Galer, Russell, 39

generally accepted principles and practices (GAPP), 84
    GAPP 6–10, 86
    GAPP 21, 86
    GAPP 18 and 19, 86
    for SWFs, 82

General Motors pension fund, 3

geographic expansion
    alignment with fund strategy, 62
    challenges of, 59–61
    goals of, 55–9, 62–3
    governance and culture, 61–2
    politics, 63
    scalability, 64
    staffing, 63

geography of finance, 7–10
    centres of global finance, 11
    large frontier cities, 10–11
    small cities on distant frontier, 11–12
    small cities on frontier, 12–13

GIC. *See* Government of Singapore Investment Corporation (GIC)

global finance, centres of, 11

global financial crisis, 16

global transparency standards, development and implementation of, 83

Google, 71

governance
    budget and performance, representation of, 26
    budget synchronization, 26
    and culture, 61–2
    investing in, 24–6
    principles of, 113–14
    rights, 41
    of satellite offices, 60

Government of Singapore Investment Corporation (GIC), 87, 94–5

Government Pension Investment Fund of Japan, 3

green infrastructure, 69

greentech strategy, 69

gross domestic product (GDP), 4

H

Harrisburg, public pension funds, 12

headline risk, 41

Hong Kong, international banks and investment services provider, 11

human capital, 128

hybrid model, 77–8

I

identity groups of financial investors, 72

IFCs. *See* international financial centres (IFCs)

IFSWF. *See* International Forum of Sovereign Wealth Funds (IFSWF)

informational advantages, 54

initial public offerings (IPOs), 71

Innovation Alliance, 74–6
    policies, 79
    principles, 77–8
    success factors, 76

innovation ecosystem, 130

institutional investment
  functional and spatial structure of,
    53
  organizations, 126
institutional investors, 30–1, 40, 42,
    44, 47–8, 55, 58, 68, 73, 77, 78,
    80–2, 85, 90, 102, 122
internal logic as bases, social *vs.*, 22–3
international balance-of-payments
    crisis, 101
international financial centres (IFCs),
    2, 7–10, 55n5, 62–3
  geographic expansion, challenges of,
    59–60
  geographic expansion, goals of, 55,
    57–8
International Forum of Sovereign
    Wealth Funds (IFSWF), 82–3,
    90
  surveys of Santiago Principles
    compliance, 84
International Monetary Fund, 84, 98,
    101
International Working Group of SWFs,
    82
investment beliefs, 17–23, 75
  development of, 20–4
Investment Company Act of 1940, 85
investment decision-making, 21
investment decisions, 18, 36, 54, 88
investment organization, 17, 34, 53,
    119, 127, 129
investment policy, elements of, 90
investment process, 104
investors, 11, 21, 34, 36, 41, 43, 49,
    54, 57, 67, 69, 72, 77, 79, 81,
    97, 103, 119–20, 122, 132
IPOs. *See* initial public offerings
    (IPOs)

J

Japanese economy, 11

K

knowledge management systems, 128
knowledge transfer, 58, 102

L

large frontier cities, 10–11
Lerner, Josh, 72
leveraging technology, 132
'linking' beliefs, 22
Local Government Officials pension
    fund, 4
local investors, 54
local market, 4, 9, 12, 59
Lockett, A., 72
London, international banks and
    investment services provider, 11
long-term institutional investors (LTIs),
    40, 67–8, 73, 75
  invest in green VC opportunities, 77–8
long-term investment, 82, 83, 87–90,
    111
long-term investors, 35, 36, 83, 88, 131
LTIs. *See* long-term institutional
    investors (LTIs)

M

macroeconomic factors, 15
macroeconomic stability, 100–1
Malaysia's Khazanah, 104
management investment committee
    (MIC), 124
management, policies of, 114–15
matrix places SDFs, 104
McNally Capital, 42, 45
MIC. *See* management investment
    committee (MIC)
mobilization, 23–4
modern portfolio theory, 21, 112
  rigid metrics of, 77
Moneyball (Lewis), 34–7
multiemployer pension fund, 4

N

national governments, 72
National Pension Service of Korea, 4
national rules and regulations, 16
NBIM. *See* Norges Bank Investment
    Management (NBIM)
New York, international banks and
    investment services provider, 11
New Zealand approach, 94
New Zealand, centres of global finance,
    10
New Zealand Superannuation Fund
    (NZSF), 74, 94, 96
non-financial centres
    in emerging markets, 60–1
    geographic expansion of, 58–61
non-local offices, 60
Norges Bank Investment Management
    (NBIM), 89
Norwegian GPF-G, 2n2, 6
Norwegian sovereign fund model, 120
NZSF. *See* New Zealand
    Superannuation Fund (NZSF)

O

Ontario Municipal Employees
    Retirement System (OMERS),
    73
'open market' foreign policy, 84
operational strategies, SDFs, 105–6
operational transparency, 93
organizational objectives, alignment
    with, 22
organizations, 62–3

P

peer-to-peer collaboration, benefits of,
    40–1
Pension Fund Association, 4
pension funds, 15, 17, 47, 74
    capitalism, 2–5

pension reserve funds, 3
performance transparency, 93
Petra Geraats's conceptual framework
    for central bank transparency,
    91
P&I/Towers Watson World 300
    (2014), 2
policies
    Innovation Alliance, 79
    of management, 114–15
    transparency, 93
political transparency, 92
politics, 63
    intersecting, 111–12
portfolio approach, 103
portfolio construction, 125
portfolio management, traditional
    models and tools of, 77
portfolio managers, 60
positive feedback control loops, 103
principal-agent problem, 30
private equity (PE) fund, 44
    investors, 103
procedural transparency, 92–3
productive efficiency, 102–6
prudent person rule, 39
public agency investor, 128
public funds, 36
    in frontier cities, 30
public pension funds, 32, 68
    and endowments, 128–9
public sector jobs, 30

R

reliance on human capital, 29
resource-constrained investors, 35
resource revenues, 100
resource-rich countries, 106
retirement-income organizations, 4
risk budget, 26
risk-conscious investors, 9
Robinson, Joan, 110

S

Santiago Principles, 82, 83, 85–8, 90
satellite in non-financial centre, 60–1
satellite office, 62, 64
    formation of, 56
Saudi Arabia, commodity exporter, 5
saving costs, 41
scalability, 60–1, 64
scepticism, 82
Schumpeter, Joseph, 110
SDF. *See* sovereign development funds
    (SDF)
seeded vehicle, 50
short-termism, 81, 91, 96
simple conceptual model, 7–8
Singapore, commodity exporter, 5
Singapore's Government Investment
    Corporation, 6
single-employer funds, 3
skilled portfolio managers, 24
skilled workers in Edmonton, 33–4
small cities
    on distant frontier, 11–12
    on frontier, 12–13
social *vs.* internal logic as bases, 22–3
sovereign development funds (SDF),
    98, 100–1
    ideal types, 99–100
    policies of management, 114–15
    potential of, 99
    principles of governance, 113–14
    productive efficiency, 101–6
    scope and possibilities of, 99
    strategic and tactical investors, 103
    strategies, 105
sovereign funds, 32, 47, 68, 81–2,
    86–7, 89
    capitalism, 5–7
    idiosyncrasies and heterogeneity of,
        88
sovereign fund solutions, 100
    distributive justice, 106–7
    intersecting politics, 111–12

macroeconomic stability, 100–1
people and organizational design,
    108–9
policies of management, 114–15
principles of governance, 113–14
principles, policies and pitfalls, 112
productive efficiency, 102–6
two views of finance, 110–11
typology, 107–8
sovereign fund transparency, five
    aspects of, 91
sovereign wealth funds (SWFs), 5–6,
    12n9, 74, 76, 81, 84, 90, 97
    behaviour in Santiago agreement, 86
    GAPP for, 82
    International Working Group of, 82
    investment decisions, 86
    public criticism of, 89
stabilization fund, 100–1
staffing, 63
standard deviation measures, 123
standardized approach for approvals,
    124
standard J-curve, 70
state-sponsored investment fund, 98
structural alpha, 103, 104
successive pension reforms, 2
sustainability, 24
SWFs. *See* sovereign wealth funds (SWFs)
Syncona Partners, 74
'synergetic' returns, 104

T

Temasek Holdings, 87
ten pillars of success, 121–33
Texas Permanent Education Fund, 6
three Gs, 31–4
TIAA-CREF, 36, 36n7
Tokyo, 11
transparency, 85, 87–90
    aspects of, 91–4
    views of, 94–5

trusted peers, 79
Type I SDF, 108–12, 117
Type II SDF, 108–9, 117

U
UC advantage, 129–31
UC ecosystem, 130
UCITS. *See* Undertakings for Collective
    Investment in Transferable
    Securities (UCITS)
UCOCIO. *See* University of
    California's Office of the
    Chief Investment Officer
    (UCOCIO)
Undertakings for Collective Investment
    in Transferable Securities
    (UCITS), 85
University of California, 130
    investment beliefs for, 23–4
University of California's Office of the
    Chief Investment Officer
    (UCOCIO), 120–1, 123–5, 129,
    132
UN PRI, 133
Urwin, Roger, 25

US administration, 72n16, 84
US Coast Guard Intelligence, 84
US endowment model, 120

V
valley of death, 69–72
valley of opportunity, 73–4
value at risk, 123
venture capital (VC), 67–9
    community, 70, 71
    disappointing returns, 71
    syndicates of, 72
    traditional model of, 70

W
wealth creation strategy, 102, 103
Wellcome Trust, 74
World Bank, 84
world's financial markets, 39
Wright, M., 72

Z
zones of uncertainty, 22